PENGUIN BOOKS

Sel[illegible]

Neil Bissoondath burst o[illegible] with the publication of h[illegible], *Digging up the Mountain*[illegible] was followed by his first novel, *A Casual Brutality*, which won instant international acclaim. *The Innocence of Age*, Bissoondath's second novel, was widely praised upon publication in 1992. Born in Trinidad, Neil Bissoondath has lived in Canada since 1973.

SELLING ILLUSIONS

The Cult of Multiculturalism in Canada

NEIL BISSOONDATH

Penguin Books

PENGUIN BOOKS
Published by the Penguin Group
Penguin Books Canada Ltd, 10 Alcorn Avenue, Toronto, Ontario, Canada M4V 3B2
Penguin Books Ltd, 27 Wrights Lane, London W8 5TZ, England
Penguin Books USA Inc., 375 Hudson Street, New York, New York 10014, U.S.A.
Penguin Books Australia Ltd, Ringwood, Victoria, Australia
Penguin Books (NZ) Ltd, 182-190 Wairau Road, Auckland 10, New Zealand

Penguin Books Ltd, Registered Offices: Harmondsworth, Middlesex, England

Published in Penguin Books, 1994

10 9 8 7 6 5 4 3 2 1

Manufactured in Canada

Canadian Cataloguing in Publication Data

Bissoondath, Neil, 1955-
Selling illusions: the cult of multiculturalism in Canada

ISBN 0-14-023878-6

1. Multiculturalism - Canada. 2. Minorities - Government policy - Canada. I. Title.

FC105.M8B5 1994 305.8'00971 C94-931894-9
F1035.A1B5 1994

For the in-laws:
Pamela
Charles

And for the next generation:
Richia & Brendan
Niran & Veaan
Élyssa

The world is full of illusion.
We carry nemesis inside us,
but we are not excused.

Robert Stone,
"The Reason for Stories"
Harper's, June 1988

Contents

SELLING ILLUSIONS

One

Glimpses Beneath the Surface

The results of the polls came as a shock to many.

The first, commissioned by the Canadian Council of Christians and Jews and conducted by Decima Research, was reported by *The Globe and Mail* in this way on December 14, 1993:

CANADIANS WANT MOSAIC TO MELT, SURVEY FINDS

Respondents believe immigrants should adopt Canada's values

Most Canadians believe the multicultural mosaic isn't working and should be replaced by a cultural melting pot, says a survey released today.

About 72 percent of respondents believe that the long-standing image of Canada as a nation of communities, each ethnic and racial group preserving its identity with the help of government policy, must give way to the U.S. style of cultural absorption.

The survey...found Canadians are "increasingly intolerant" of demands made by ethnic groups, and are frustrated by "the lack of conformity" in Canadian society.

> "Canadians report a preference for 'homogenization' of the society through adoption by immigrants of Canada's values and way of life," the survey says.[1]

The *Montreal Gazette*, reporting on the same poll, on the same day, chose to highlight not the actual results of the poll but an interpretation of them:

> CANADIANS HARBOR 'LATENTLY RACIST' ATTITUDES: POLL
>
> Most reject idea of cultural diversity, saying ethnics should try to fit in[2]

However, each paper reported one important statistic in a different way. Fifty-four percent of Canadians, said the *Globe*, "believe the current immigration policy 'provides for a good balance of people,'" while the *Gazette*/Southam News report claimed instead that 54 percent "believe current immigration policy allows 'too many people of different races and cultures.'" (The *Globe* puts this figure at 41 percent.) Both figures are high, and should have been surprising to no one with even the most rudimentary sense of the shifting undercurrents in Canadian society.

The second poll, conducted for the federal government by Ekos Research Associates Inc., received front-page treatment in the *Globe* on March 10, 1994. "Four in ten Canadians," it discovered, "believe there are too many members of visible minorities [in Canada], singling out Arabs, blacks and Asians for discrimination."[3] Toronto, a city with an immigrant population of 38 percent, turned out to be the intolerance capital of Canada, with a stunning 67 percent saying there were too many immigrants, up 21 percent from the results of a poll conducted just two years before.[4] Even so, it was pointed out that "nearly three-quarters of those surveyed agreed that a mix of cultures makes Canada a more attractive place to live."

We are a country addicted to lengthy and laborious study. There is hardly a subject we have not polled or Royal-Commissioned to death. We respond avidly to the most intimate of questions. We believe in boards of inquiry, months of testimony, stacks of research papers, final reports too thick and multi-volumed to be read by any but the most avid—not to mention public-opinion surveys confusing even to seasoned reporters.

The effort itself seems to exhaust us: the knowledge, gained at great intellectual effort and financial expense, sits on shelves, glowing like some long-forgotten radioactive waste material. Or perhaps the endless studies simply satisfy the need we have to create the right appearance: we acknowledge the problem, whatever it may be, and then proceed to study it and study it and study it...all to little or no effect.

At the very least, one thinks, we should by now have acquired a little self-knowledge. But self-knowledge does not come from study alone. It comes from a knowledge of history, from self-examination and from open and vigorous debate, a candid exchange of opposing points of view. Too often in this country we gravitate towards the superficial, and so polls that claim to take our measure can still surprise and dismay us. We are suspicious of debate, anxious about the truths it might reveal. We prefer regulation, the imposition of legal barriers, in our pursuit of peace, order and good government. We prefer, then, a loaded silence.

And few silences are as loaded in this country as the one encasing the cult that has grown up around our policy of multiculturalism.

In reaction to the Decima poll, Sheila Finestone, secretary of state for multiculturalism, is quoted in the *Gazette*/Southam News report as affirming that "the Liberals have no plans to retreat from a multicultural policy. Instead, she promised to give education in multicultural issues a higher profile." Ms. Finestone then went on to attribute some blame to the faltering economy (which encourages a search for scapegoats) and to racial notions encouraged by Preston Manning and the Reform Party. Like so many others, Ms. Finestone had no hesitation in equating opposition to multicultural policy with racist sentiment.

A month later, when MPs from the Bloc Québécois and the Reform Party criticized federal multicultural funding for encouraging ethnic ghettos through grants to ethnic communities, they were accused, first, of wishing to import the U.S. "melting pot" approach to Canada and, second, of xenophobia.[5] Attempts by the Reform Party to put multiculturalism on the public agenda are routinely rejected with accusations of racism.

It is probably essential that I declare here my complete independence of all political parties. When it comes to the Reform Party in particular—the only official, national party that has dared criticize multiculturalism policy in public—my attitude is at best suspicious. Reform strikes me as a party that suffers from an astounding lack of social generosity and counts among its membership too many who are either racially minded or, to coin a phrase, knowledge-challenged.

But the countering of criticism with accusation is a tactic not unfamiliar to me. My own attempts to contribute to public discourse have been met with nervous silence, a certain vilification and, finally, the explicit demand at one conference that I *Shut up!*, since criticism of multicultural policy, I was told, served only "to encourage racists like the Reform Party." The cumulative effect of such an attitude is to put what is essentially government public policy out of bounds; it is to afford it an exclusivity extended not even to the country's security apparatus, which is itself subject to constant scrutiny.

Anyone critical of multicultural policy, then, is immediately branded a racist. And if one happens to be, as I am, a "person of colour," one is then graced with words such as "sell-out," "traitor" and "Uncle Tom" from "ethnic" defenders with a stake in the system and from mainstream defenders who expect a little more gratitude. Many are they in this country who fear a serious examination of multiculturalism, its policies and its consequences. Many are they who will resort to a chorus of vilification to protect their sacred turf.

This reaction, I suspect, has more than a little to do with the psychology of the True Believer, who sees Canada's present multiculturalism policy—generous and laudable, prompted by an inclusive vision of humanity—as the only one possible. But no policy can be written in stone; no policy is immune to evolution. When its defenders come to view a policy as without alternative; when they come to view honest criticism as mere attack; when they come to view critics as enemies, they also indulge in a logic that has led, elsewhere, to unfortunate consequences.

An example—and by this I suggest an intellectual parallel—is the old Soviet attitude towards dissent. If Communism was the perfect political system, the logic ran, then critics of it were, by definition, mentally unstable, for only the insane would criticize perfection. It was therefore incumbent on the state to villify such people and confine them to mental institutions. Just as the Soviet state responded to criticism by branding its critics mentally ill, so the Canadian multicultural apparatus responds to criticism by branding its critics racist.

It is an easy and, from an ideological point of view, logical way of dismissing uncomfortable truths. And this is what lends to multiculturalism aspects of the cult: the rules are established, you question them at your peril.

A free and healthy society must be wary of all orthodoxies, whether those of the oppressor or the oppressed, of the exploiter or the exploited, of the mainstream or the marginalized. Orthodoxy is itself a form of tyranny, with ideology—political, social, racial, financial—as its angry deity. Multiculturalism has, over the years, acquired aspects of a holy cow for many, a cash cow for some. Both are dangerous creatures. Standing on consecrated ground, they resent being disturbed and, when challenged, are inclined to bite. But a society that wishes to remain healthy and to grow must, from time to time, stare the holy cows down; it must probe and question them, and decide on their merits and usefulness. To fail to do so is to atrophy.

There are many ways of approaching a laudable end. It is incumbent on those who seek it—the end, in this case, being a truly pluralistic society—to define their vision with words weightier than vacuous expressions of goodwill. It is also vital that they not settle into the kind of self-righteous complacency that summarily rejects criticism, for to do so not only calls their vision into disrepute but also proves inimical to the fabric of the society that vision seeks to serve.

Multiculturalism is an emotional subject. It reaches into our past and our present, into the core of ourselves. It engages all that has shaped us. It touches us where we are the most vulnerable and the most self-protective.

For this reason, this book does not claim to be an objective examination of multiculturalism. A subject so personal, one that cuts so close to the bone, defies objectivity. It is, then, a personal attempt to grapple with a policy which, from my earliest days in this country, has presented itself as a social cornerstone; it is an attempt to look at where we are and how we got here.

The question of the financial costs of multiculturalism does not preoccupy me. The federal government dispenses less than $30 million per year to the department, not an insignificant sum but one that does not particularly stand out among government expenditures. Former prime minister Mulroney, after all, spent more than that on a presidential-style aircraft.

Multiculturalism interests me rather as an official government policy and, more particularly, as a government-sanctioned mentality: as a way of looking at life and at the world; for the ways in which it shapes our sense of self and our place in human society. I am interested in the effects of multiculturalism, then, on our individual and collective selves.

Nor, let me add, does this book claim to be prescriptive. I am neither a literary doctor, a sociologist nor a politician. I do not pretend to have all, or any, answers, although I do offer some suggestions in the same spirit that I offer criticism: as a way of contributing to the necessary discussion on the shaping of an increasingly unhappy and divided land.

Two

Generational Drift: Getting Here

The story of my families' migrations begins over a hundred years ago, in an Indian state gripped then, as now, in the kind of poverty that not only demeans the present but makes nonsense of notions of the future.

The people who would turn out to be my ancestors packed their meagre belongings and set off on an adventure that would take them to a place of greater promise half a world away. After an arduous overland journey to the Indian port city of Calcutta, they boarded a ship for a journey of many months to the small Caribbean island of Trinidad, then a British colony inhabited in the main by emancipated African slaves, former slave-owners and a smattering of Chinese, with whom the British had unsuccessfully tried to replace the slave labour.

My ancestors were not slaves; they were not, at least, the legal property of those for whom they laboured in the sugarcane fields. They were indentured labourers who had signed five-year contracts, which promised a pay-off of either land in Trinidad or money and passage back to India. Theirs were lives of great hardship most certainly, but lives, too, begun with advantages denied the former slaves to whom liberation meant that most terrifying of freedoms, the freedom of nothingness.

My ancestors and their compatriots, offered a new chance by the exploitative vicissitudes of empire, were not long in establishing villages and a way of life reflective of the ones they had left behind: adobe huts, vegetable gardens, rice paddies, all within the parentheses of Hinduism or Islam. Trinidad, then, was that kind of place, a colony in which the native population had long been wiped out and onto which could be inscribed the ethnic strokes of colonialism.

Time and distance did its inevitable work. As India receded, as the new life acquired its own dynamic, the transported people of the subcontinent learned to think of this new land as home.

My families—the Bissoondaths, the Naipauls—chose to remain at the end of their period of indenture. They had found success, and success through hardship is a commodity not easily surrendered.

Trinidad is a small island that sits just off the coast of Venezuela. Geography gave the island a hot climate, rich soil and oil reserves both on and off shore. History made the island a British colony disdainful of those who did not belong: despite the proximity of Latin America, contacts were few, influence minimal. Even the French islands of Martinique and Guadeloupe, geographically close, similar in historical experience, hardly entered our consciousness.

Then, on August 31, 1962, Trinidad became an independent nation under the British crown. I was seven years old, and my memories of that grand time are few. I remember lying on a mattress at night in my grandmother's house in Port of Spain, the capital, and listening to a cacophony of ships' horns mingled with the regular crash of artillery from the newly formed military force.

At school, we each received a chocolate bar and a little gilded medal, symbols of promise. And then there were the flags: the old Union Jack, which my grandfather had flown outside his store, furled and abandoned in a corner, history now; and the new, a red field dissected diagonally, from the upper left corner to the lower right, by a wide black band bordered by narrow white stripes.

In the years to come, the new flag would be reproduced innumerable times in my sketch-books. It would be drawn in pencil or in ink, crayon-coloured or water-coloured, free and fluttering or ruled stiffly to scale. Beneath it, within a stylized ribbon, I would inscribe the island's new motto, "*Together We Aspire, Together We Achieve.*" The phrase appealed to me; it had a wonderful resonance, and it neatly captured the vision of hope and optimism vital to the new era.

At school, the new anthem would be drilled into us, and after more than thirty years, twenty of them in a new country, the lyrics remain as familiar to me as the alphabet:

Forged from the love of liberty
In the fires of hope and prayer ...

It was a stirring song, with just the right touch of majesty. Like the motto, it seemed to offer promises of a peaceful and productive life: visions of the varied peoples of this "cosmopolitan" island (as our teachers constantly characterized it) working together to create a new unity, multiculturalism without the name. As a youngster, I believed in the words; they spoke to the idealist in me.

When I was about ten years old, I decided to enter an island-wide painting competition in honour of the independence anniversary. My effort was poor. It was an outline of the island coloured green, flanked by the flag and failed renderings of the birds—the Scarlet Ibis, the humming-bird—that had been chosen as symbols of ourselves and the future we were to build: beauty, strength, persistence, industry. My entry, duly submitted despite my misgivings, was dull and heavy, earnest in its embrace of the new nationalism. Needless to say, it was not awarded a prize. It was not even returned.

I believe it was this disappointment in myself—in this failure of my imagination, the artistic overwhelmed by the civic—that first awoke my sense of irony. For the first time, I found myself pulling back from the phrases and symbols of social optimism, found myself beginning to measure them against the realities around me. I was, in short, beginning to grow up.

In my imagination the friends of my childhood remain young. Their faces come to me frozen in adolescence; it has been decades since I have seen any of them. Only through the greatest effort of imagination can I ascribe grey hair and wrinkles to their youthful looks.

We were a varied group, both racially (black, white, Chinese, Indian, mulatto) and religiously (Presbyterian, Roman Catholic, Hindu, Moslem).

There was my namesake, Neil, gentle and always smiling. And Wayne, a soccer player whose talents, in a larger land, might have led to a career; Brian, whose angers would lead him to radical Marxism and Black Power; Dave, whose intelligence would take him to Oxford and a diplomatic career. There was Andrew, from England; Vivek, from India; Reza, from Oman. There was Richard, who would die of a drug overdose; and Frank, who would die in a car accident. And so many more ...

In the rhetoric of the time, we were the future leaders of the new nation. We were absorbed by chemistry and physics, mathematics and geography, English, French, Spanish and, above all, by cricket. Race, religion, politics did not seem to matter. They *should* not have mattered. But, inevitably, they did.

On the verge of adolescence, Zaid and I were, for a time, deskmates. We were friends. We played together in the dusty schoolyard and, even though we were not of the faith, sang the Presbyterian hymns at the morning worship. Zaid was Muslim, I was Hindu, but this meant only that our families celebrated different religious festivals: Mohammed and Krishna exercised no influence on our friendship. Yet, when Zaid's father suddenly died, a silence descended between us. He had no words to express his loss, and the language of condolence was unknown to me. I knew that Hindus cremated their dead, and I wondered what Muslims did. But my curiosity seemed an intrusion. I could not bring myself to ask. Our friendship ended in a wordless ballet of pained glances.

On the verge of adulthood, Shaffique and I were friends. We talked together during the hot lunch periods and, because we were not of the faith, stood in respectful silence while our classmates said the "Hail, Mary." Shaffique was Muslim and I was Hindu but, as with Zaid, our religions exercised no influence on our friendship. Until, that is, late in 1971, when war erupted between Pakistan and India over the breakaway state of East Pakistan, now Bangladesh. The war and its merits was, like Vietnam, like Northern Ireland, a topic of vigorous discussion at school. For me, though, debate came to an abrupt end one morning when, as I expressed support for Indian intervention in the face of reported massacres by the Pakistani army, Shaffique, who had been eavesdropping on the conversation, whipped around and, with great indignation, declared that Hindus should keep their damned noses out of Muslim affairs.

This advent into the personal stunned me into wordlessness, and once more a friendship ended in a strained silence, but this time with a vision of schism never anticipated. I had thought us beyond such loyalties, had thought us people freed of ancient divisiveness by new circumstances. Just as I had never seen Shaffique as representative of his religion or his ancestral land, so I never saw myself as defending the interests of my (official) religion or ancestral land.

Other schisms began to make themselves apparent. It became clear as I grew older and developed an interest in politics that those who, in 1962, had offered promises of "aspiring" and "achieving" together had conceived of only a narrow togetherness. They engaged readily in the politics of race. The island divided itself into two camps, the People's National Movement, which was largely the party for blacks, and the Democratic Labour Party, which was largely the party for Indians. It was considered scandalous for anyone to break racial solidarity by voting for the other party: it was our island version of apartheid, as virile, as divisive, as insidious. We, the descendants of former slaves and the descendants of indentured labourers, had learnt racial distrust. We had acquired—or perhaps just acknowledged and institutionalized—a sense of racial unease.

A 1990 census of the island revealed that the population of 1.2 million was 43 percent African and 40 percent East Indian, with the rest coming from a variety of racial and cultural groups. And yet, in a place where truth was formless, where one was taught to dismiss nothing and to distrust everything, even so simple an undertaking as a population count could lead to anxiety. Some years ago, shortly after an earlier census, Indians whispered to each other that their numbers had actually surpassed 50 percent but that the black-controlled government had, through fear of numerical inferiority, suppressed the figure. There was, I felt, something tragic about that rumour. It indicated a certain paranoia, seemed a sign of despair. And it made it clear that, contrary to the popular claims, we were no happy island in the sun.

We were even incapable of playing together without mutterings of dissatisfaction. No selection of the Trinidadian or West Indian cricket teams could be made without a "deserving" Indian being left off because—so the whispers went—of his race.

But it was at the island's annual carnival that the falseness of the notions of play, of fun in the sun, became most explicit. Many aspirations, and much time, money and effort, are invested in the carnival. It is spectacle on the grand scale, a two-day street party that effectively shuts down the island. It is as brilliant as Rio's, but more imaginative and less controlled: anyone, local or tourist, can join in. So it was with a certain dismay that my ironic eye began to discern divisions not readily apparent: that while people of every race participated, they did so in little pockets of homogeneity, blacks with blacks, Indians with Indians, whites with whites. Only the tourists, ignorant of indigenous tensions, felt free to mingle.

And yet, as painful as social hypocrisy may be, hypocrisy in private cuts more deeply. There is no defence against it, no easy shrug of *C'est la vie.* It slices into the soul. There is in youth no recognition or acceptance of the personal hypocrisies acquired through life and circumstance. The ironic eye did not stop at the larger society around me; it applied itself with equal dismay to the more intimate circles within which I lived my daily life.

The phrases, overheard in the conversations of intelligent and educated people, marked themselves with the particular ferocity that keeps them fresh in my mind after many years: "If a nigger is a nigger, what you can do about it?"; "I couldn't let him continue in that karate class after I saw the teacher was a big black niggerman"; "She's nice, eh—for a Black."

It was difficult in the grip of dismay to know how to respond to one relative's disdain for people of mixed Indian/black race while admiring the fairer skin of Indian/white issue; difficult to know how to intervene when social conversation included fluid references to "nigs" and unquestioned distrust of Muslims. When stern arguments were made that blacks were congenitally incapable of running governments—that incompetence and corruption were endemic to them—I would point to the undeniable chaos of India: I have yet to meet an Indian willing to draw racial conclusions from that nightmare.

But the only time I recall exploding was the day a New York business agent, a man hitherto well liked, made a small shipping mistake and became, in a moment of anger, a "dirty Jew." The explosion was prompted by years of uneasy silence, finally broken by my disbelief that the only Jew known to this man could be so easily dismissed by racial epithet. The defence left me speechless with despair: "I didn't mean anything by it. It's just an expression."

Just an expression. The unexamined acceptance of a racial vision, life filtered through the colour of skin and conventional stereotype, has never struck me as in any way benign. It is a vision that proceeds from differences, from that which separates, disregarding that which unites.

It was never explicitly said that black or Muslim school friends were not welcome in our homes. They *were*, at least theoretically, but the only blacks I recall at the grand parties were the policemen sometimes hired to provide security from the growing violence of the island. The limits were implicit.

A recent conversation with a relative is revealing. Denying that her parents were in any way racist, she pointed out that they welcomed all her friends to their home. Her black friends too? Yes, her black friends too: they just made it clear *she wasn't to marry any of them.*

Growing up in Trinidad was for me, on both the social and personal levels, an exercise in dissatisfaction. But it was not so for everyone.

My mother, born and educated in Port of Spain, a woman widely read and travelled, always swore that she would never leave Trinidad, no matter how difficult life became. Although she enjoyed London, New York, Paris, Caracas, Rio de Janeiro, and despite her particular fondness for Venice, Trinidad was her home in ways I could not appreciate, a place to which she was tied in ways that were to me frustrating because they were inscrutable. She had grown to feel herself linked to the place, just as I had grown to feel myself alienated from it. The intimacy of her feeling was not one I could engage. There had been, I felt, too many betrayals.

The world is full of stories of immigrants struggling to make places for themselves in new lands. They tend to be stories of hardship and debilitating compromise, loneliness and drift: stories, then, of roots severed, souls exiled, best captured by someone who once suggested that there were few sights sadder than that of a brown man in an overcoat.

And yet my own story was nothing of the kind.

At the age of eighteen, I left Trinidad for good. I went to a city, Toronto, about which I knew nothing, in a country, Canada, about which I knew little.

Like many newcomers, I am often asked why I chose Canada, the question always posed by native-born Canadians in such a way as to suggest that one has somehow made a dreadful mistake in coming here. The answer is simple. Canada had been recommended to me by a respected relative as an effective compromise between the two other possible destinations, England and the United States. It was not my own sparse knowledge of the country that brought me here.

I had studied Canadian geography in high school, knew of the Canadian Shield and the St. Lawrence River. I had heard of Yonge Street, but it was just a name; of Winnipeg, but only because an uncle had attended university there. I had some years before seen grainy television film of FLQ terrorists being driven in convoy to an airport, but that too had remained with me without context.

And yet, the new city, the new country, quickly acquired texture, took on shape, became real. Became, in short order, my home.

Call it luck. I was at university, in an atmosphere that was not the larger society but an approximation of it. A university campus, particularly one as physically isolated as York University's in Toronto, is to a certain extent a protected, protective, ready-made community. For a newcomer to the country, it is a centre of transition, a viewpoint from which to learn, for better or for worse, the make-up and workings of the new society.

Toronto, large, fast, with a population almost three times larger than that of Trinidad at that time, proved exciting in some ways, intimidating in others. Living near the university campus in the suburb of Downsview, I had for a while only the vaguest concept of a "downtown," of a city grander than my drab surroundings. But this did not matter. I was experiencing a sense of freedom long anticipated, savouring new possibilities, devouring books, magazines, films, all the openings to the world denied me in Trinidad.

At the university, I came by friends easily and, through them, discovered the city, a place of remarkable diversity, a place where—as another newcomer described it—

you were simply "part of the difference." And yet it was also a place unsettled in a kind of adolescence. The city seemed proud of what it was becoming; it had shrugged off the torpor of the fifties, was hungrily reaching for the social and cultural excitements that had swept the continent in the sixties, only it was doing so without the shadows that had darkened the streets of other large North American cities. It was proud of being Toronto the Good, the City that Works: anyone could walk in safety anywhere at anytime.

And yet, at the same time, there was an unmistakable sense in the controlled ferment that the city wasn't quite sure what to make of itself. Some streets, with their New York-style boutiques and their New York-style bistros, palpitated with a desire to imitate, like teenagers trying on different styles in pursuit of their true selves. This mimicry, often characteristic of a colonized people, was at the time incomprehensible to me; it seemed at odds with the reigning confidence and optimism. I was not yet sufficiently familiar with the city (and the country) to see that this imitation was indeed part of a decolonization process: the Britishness that had for so long characterized Canada was quickly giving way to a new North Americanness, or at least to a version of it.

But a big city can be misleading. It can give the impression that it defines the country: people familiar with only Toronto or Calgary or Montreal will speak of life "in Canada." I had grown up in a tiny island hemmed in by the sea, and it was a while before the sheer massiveness of Canada impressed itself on me. The mind only slowly accommodates such physical immensity. It may have taken so simple a thing as a plane flight. How amazing it was that one could fly for hours, disembark into a markedly different climate and still have no need of a passport. The realization offered a particular, and peculiar, joy to someone accustomed to an idea of limitation both physical and psychic. The mere size of the land seemed to speak to its possibilities.

Gradually, I discovered other, more prosaic reasons for pride in my adopted country. It was in the simplest of things (fire trucks that arrived within minutes of a call and not five or six hours later) and also in the grander things, well-kept secrets (outside the country) such as the Canadian commitment to a social safety net and the Canadian zeal for peacekeeping duties in dangerous parts of the world.

And it began to be clear that Canada was not, as many both inside and outside chose to view it, merely an imitation America. Its history was different, less bloody, and so less prone to mythologizing, the people more inclined to peace than pacification. I began to see Canadians as people who viewed the world in less voracious terms than Americans, believers in compromise and negotiation who yet had the courage to be firm when necessary.

In the end, then, I got the sense of a people at ease with themselves, in charge of their own destiny, a land of immigrants and descendents of immigrants given another chance by history and determined to construct a new and fruitful tomorrow. If many outside Canada (save those in need of succour or safe haven) frequently seemed unaware of its existence, this was likely due to its citizens' preference for compromise over confrontation: anonymity is not always a bad thing.

The country offered hope, then, without banging me over the head with its own glories: my newcomer anxieties—how will this adventure play itself out?—quickly gave way to a sense that this was a land worthy of commitment. So it was puzzling to me that Canadians were struggling with self-definition, as if they keenly felt the lack of a national image—an image that, like all stereotypes, would be useful only to bigots and bad comedians.

If the York University campus was a safe haven from which to discover the pleasures of Canada, though, it was also the place where I first encountered reasons for unease.

York operates on a college system. New students choose, or are assigned to, one of the various colleges on the campus. Unfamiliar with the system, ignorant of the purposes behind the individual colleges, I allowed myself to be assigned to Bethune College.

Familiarity with the college brought a certain dismay. Bethune College, named in honour of Dr. Norman Bethune, is an institution devoted to Third World studies; it had a certain reputation for left-wing radicalism. The reason for my dismay was simple: my major was to be French language and literature. The bilingual Glendon College, my logical "home," was never mentioned. I can only assume that I was enrolled at Bethune in part because I had come from a Third World country and in part because my adviser assumed that I would be most comfortable in an environment where a high percentage of students were, like me, non-white. It was an assuredly benign assumption, one made with the best of intentions, but also with no regard to my personal beliefs or intellectual interests. My adviser, then, had looked at me through the lens of her own stereotype and guided me according to the presumed comforts of "sticking with your own."

Although I was not at first aware of it, the concept of "sticking with your own" was just then in vogue at York. This became clear the moment you entered the main cafeteria at Central Square in the massive concrete bunker of the Ross Building. It was large and brashly lit, institutional in character, a place for feeding oneself rather than enjoying a meal. I remember it as a loud and busy place, brash with the sounds of trays and cutlery roughly handled, of a multitude of voices blended into a steady roar.

And yet, it seemed a benign atmosphere, friendly in an impersonal way. The controlled chaos offered an anonymity that would ease the task of inserting oneself, of fitting in. Or so it seemed at first.

Chaos is always subtly ordered, and it did not require a very discerning eye to decode the chaos of the Central Square cafeteria. Indeed, a map could be drawn, various sections coloured in to denote defined areas. To highlight, for instance, the table at which Chinese students congregated behind a wall of Cantonese; or the tables over in the corner protected by the raucous enthusiasm of West Indian accents; or the table more subtly framed by yarmulkes and Star of David pendants.

To approach any of these tables was to intrude on a clannish exclusivity. It was to challenge the unofficially designated territory of tables parcelled out so that each group, whether racially, culturally or religiously defined, could enjoy its little enclave, its own little "homeland," so to speak, protected by unspoken prerogatives.

The idea of "sticking with your own" was reinforced by various student organizations, many of which were financially assisted by the university. Controversy arose at one point when an application for membership in the Black Students' Federation was received from a student—a writer for the campus newspaper, as it turned out—whose skin colour seemed to disqualify him. Questions arose: Was being black a prerequisite for belonging to the Black Students' Federation? Or was a commitment to the issues raised by the association sufficient justification for belonging? Just how relevant was skin colour, how relevant cultural background, how relevant political belief?

A hint of the complexity of the question may be discerned in a story once told to me by a friend. One afternoon, he stopped in at his favourite coffee house in Toronto's Kensington Market, a small place brightly decorated in the tropical style. It featured reggae music and the rich Blue Mountain coffee from Jamaica. As he sipped his coffee, he eavesdropped on a conversation at the table behind him, three young men, evidently musicians, discussing their next gig. My friend understood little of what was said—their thick Jamaican accents made their words undecipherable—but he enjoyed listening to their speech in the same way that he enjoyed the sounds of reggae. Cup empty, he rose to leave. On his way out he glanced at the men and with delight saw, as he put it, "one black guy with dreadlocks and two white guys with blond hair and blue eyes." An encounter, then, with the wickedness of history. He left the coffee house thrilled at abandoning the wreckage of a stereotype.

The issue at York was eventually settled by the decision to admit the white student to the Federation—not on the grounds that race was irrelevant but that, as an organization financially assisted by the university, it had to respect the university's regulations prohibiting discrimination on the grounds of race and colour. I did not belong to the Federation, but the resolution was pleasing anyway, even though there was a tincture of discomfort at the way in which it had come about: through technicality, and not through the application of principle. None of the real questions had been grappled with, none answered.

Questions of segregation and exclusivity kept raising their heads. One day a Jewish friend invited me to join him for coffee in the Jewish Students' Federation lounge.

I was reluctant—the lounge seemed to me governed by even stronger proscriptions than the table in the cafeteria—but he insisted. As he fixed us each a coffee, he said in a voice clearly intended for others in the room that I should feel free to help myself from the coffee-machine at any time. And then he added in strained tones that the lounge, provided by the university, was open to all: I was to ignore anyone who tried to stop me. It was in this way that he sought to make me part of unsuspected internecine tensions, while publicly declaring his own position.

The issues made me wary: I neither joined the Black Students' Federation nor revisited the Jewish Students' Federation lounge. I learned instead to keep my distance from the tables that would have welcomed me not as an individual but as an individual of a certain skin colour, with a certain accent, with a certain assumed cultural outlook—the tables that would have welcomed me not for *who* I was and for what I could do but for *what* I was and for what they presumed I represented. I had not come here, I decided, in order to join a ghetto.

Alone in a new land, I faced inevitable questions. Questions about my past and my present, about the land left behind and the land newly found, about the nature of this society and my place in it. At eighteen, about to embark on a new life, I felt these to be weighty issues.

For many people at those cafeteria tables, though, these were questions of no great importance. They were almost aggressive in dismissing any discomfort they might have experienced by flaunting the only government policy that seemed to arouse no resentment: Canada as a multicultural land. Officially. Legally. Here, they insisted, you did not have to change. Here you could—indeed, it was your duty to—remain what you were. None of this American melting-pot nonsense, none of this remaking yourself to fit your new circumstances: you did not have to adjust to the society, the society was obligated to accommodate itself to you.

An attractive proposal, then, a policy that excused much and required little effort. And yet I found myself not easily seduced.

The problem was that I had come in search of a new life and a new way of looking at the world, "to expand my horizons" (to use a cliché) from the narrow perspectives of my youth in Trinidad. I had no desire to transport here life as I had known it: this seemed to me particularly onerous baggage with which to burden one's shoulders. Beyond this, though, the very act of emigration had already changed me. I was no longer the same person who had boarded the aircraft in Trinidad bound for Toronto: I had brought with me not the attitudes of the tourist but those of someone embarking on an adventure that would forever change his life. This alone was a kind of psychological revolution.

Multiculturalism, as perceived by those at whom it was most explicitly aimed, left me with a certain measure of discomfort.

At the end of my first university year, I returned to Trinidad to visit my parents. It wasn't long before I was impatient to get back to Toronto. This had to do in part with the realization that, even after so short a time, old friends had become new strangers, and that old places had remained simply old places. More importantly, though, the desire to return had to do with me and with the life I had begun constructing in my adopted city. I relished the freedom this life offered, the liberation of the anonymity of the big city. I had made new friends—some of them from among "my own kind," some not—and had found all the books, magazines and films denied me in Trinidad. I had, for the first time in my life, found a place other than my parents' house that I wished to call home: a place where I could be myself.

Sharing this with those who wished me to bolster their ethnic bastion in Toronto made me distinctly unpopular. I was seen as a kind of traitor, unwilling to play the game by indulging in a life best described as "Caribbean North." If there was any alienation, it came not from the society at large but from those who saw themselves as the front-line practitioners of multiculturalism. By establishing cultural and racial exclusivity, they were doing their bit to preserve the multicultural character of the country, while I, seeking to go beyond the confines of my cultural heritage, was seen as acting counter to those interests.

To put it succinctly, they coveted the segregated tables of the cafeteria, while I sought a place at tables that would accommodate a greater variety.

For a long time now, I have thought of Trinidad as simply the place where I was born; the place where I got my early education; the place where my parents died. After half a lifetime away from the island, I have no emotional attachment left, and my interest in its events is no different from my interest in events in China or Russia or Botswana: analytical, intellectual. I miss nothing, am prey to no nostalgia. I have neither axes to grind nor scores to settle. When I am travelling abroad, when I feel myself in need of comfort, security, familiarity, it is this country—its air, its sounds, its smells, the textures of its light—that I long for. It is here, everywhere, that I find the comforts of home: in its ungraspable vastness, its diversity of geography, its climate and peoples, its yet unformed face, which is itself both a warning and a possibility.

In the end, I am as at home in Montreal as I am in

Vancouver, in Toronto as I am in Quebec City, in English as in French. Nowhere have I felt myself a stranger. Alienation, expatriation, exile: they are just words to me now, not personal issues; they are intellectual concepts that fascinate precisely because they are so distant.

My history. my past, my "roots"—the people, places and events that have shaped me—are an integral part of myself. Just as no one can take them away, so I cannot rid myself of them. This does not mean, though, that I must be their prisoner. Notions of the past, historical and personal, can be either a cloak of perpetual resentment or the centre that helps individuals understand who they are and where they stand in the world. They can consume from within, or they can shape the values and beliefs that show the way forward. The past is the past; it must be acknowledged and understood, but it cannot be undone. Yesterday's humiliations are just that, *yesterday*'s humiliations, and to nurture them is to indulge in the fruitlessness of vengeance.

History, roots, the various people we have been, are today and will be tomorrow all come together to offer a definition of the self. They form a personal complexity that derives from but is not beholden to any particular set of values, events or circumstances. They are the knowledge of unspoken wisdoms that can free the individual to be him- or herself and, so, insofar as possible, unassailable.

My own roots are portable, adaptable, the source of a personal freedom that allows me to feel "at home" in a variety of places and languages without ever forgetting who I am or what brought me here. My roots travel with me, in my pocket, as it were, there to guide or succour me as need be. They are, in the end, the sum of my experience, historical, familial and personal. They are, in the end, my sense of self.

We can change homes. We can grow attached to new places, new people, new ways of doing things and looking at the world. What we cannot do, indeed, what we must never attempt to do, is forget the homes of the past, for they too have shaped us.

I was born a Trinidadian. I was brought up a Trinidadian. But that was a long time ago. I am no longer Trinidadian. I have not been Trinidadian for many years. I do not share the hopes, fears, joys and views of Trinidadians. I am not familiar with the thoughts that move them, the ideas that stir them.

The fact remains, though, that Trinidad's motto, "Together We Aspire, Together We Achieve," humanitarian in vision, universal in philosophy, betrayed by so many people in so many ways, still speaks to me. It offers a sentiment that I believe worthy of preservation, worthy of the land that, more than twenty years after my departure from Trinidad, I have learned to call home.

Three

Beginnings

Our memory of the past must be faithful to the future if it is to act as stimulus for the present.

Naim Kattan
Language & Society
Fall 1987[1]

So complete has been their engagement with the society both personally and professionally that they seem to have been here forever. That there is nothing parochial about the Ignatieff family is not surprising. That they are defined by a becoming cosmopolitanism is no surprise either. The surprise is that they should have come so quickly to embody a kind of Canadianism: an idea of public service, the life of the mind.

Revolution drove them from their homeland, turning generations of achievement and service into history and family legend.

Splendid regal uniforms gave way to more modest civilian dress, a certain wealth to a certain poverty. The excitements of imperial service were replaced by the uncertainties of a less structured existence. They ended up, after some meandering, in Montreal, stateless, penniless, admitted to Canada as agricultural labourers.

Count Paul Ignatieff and his wife Natasha—he, once a reform-minded member of Tsar Nicholas II's cabinet; she, born a princess of the accomplished Mestchersky family—determined that there would be no surrender to straitened circumstances. They insisted to their sons—Nicholas, Vladimir, Alec, Lionel and George—that "the past was the past and that they must not end up like so many émigrés driving taxis and keeping their bags packed for the return journey to Petersburg."[2] Neither did they try "to clamp their children within an émigré ghetto or to insist on Russian brides."[3]

Paul and Natasha died before the end of World War II, she in August 1944, he a year later. They died in their modest cottage at Upper Melbourne, Quebec, far from the landscape and circumstances of their birth. But the attitudes they had inculcated in their sons were not without effect. Nicholas joined the University of Toronto as a Soviet expert intent on combatting anti-Soviet sentiment. Vladimir became a soils chemist, spending three decades with the Food and Agricultural Organization in Africa and Asia. Alec, a mining engineer, ended up running the Department of Mines in Canada's Ministry of Energy, while Lionel, in many ways the least reconciled to exile, obtained a doctorate and taught Russian literature at the University of Western Ontario. George, whose working life began at sixteen as an axeman in the forests of British Columbia, won a Rhodes scholarship to Oxford and eventually developed into the consummate diplomat, his talents put to the service not of the Tsar, as they probably would have been had history been different, but of the government of Canada. The adjective "distinguished" is a word now almost synonymous with the man and his life.

The story of the Ignatieff family is not always a happy one—it includes its share of hardship, tensions and schism. It is, in the romance of its details, extraordinary, not your typical refugee or émigré story; but, then, there may be no such thing except in a tale shorn, always unjustly, of its particularities, a human story without the humanity, a story disembodied. Nor is the story of the Ignatieff family particularly unique: it has been repeated throughout the century, countless times and to varying degrees, in many countries.

Some may say that the Ignatieff boys were privileged. They benefited from a superior education, their parents having scrimped and saved the tuition to Lower Canada College. It could be said that they benefited from the efforts of Natasha, who, in particular, provided an indispensable stability at home, a sense of a centre when all else had been lost. It could be said that they found strength in a knowledge of their past, a knowledge of their own worth unavailable to many.

It cannot be denied, though, that they were boys who grew into men who worked at their opportunities. If the Ignatieffs are seen, today, as part of the Canadian élite, it is not because of birthright or family fortune: it is because, through effort and achievement, they have made it so.

But there is, too, another aspect of the story, of every such story. For all of this—the uncertainties, the struggles, the failures and the successes—took place within a certain context, that of the country to which the family had come.

When Paul and Natasha arrived in Montreal, they were officially stateless, flotsam of history.

When they died, they died as official citizens of Canada.

When they were buried, they were placed in a soil to which they belonged as much as it belonged to them.

Almost half a century after the death of grandparents

he never knew in the flesh but whom, through history, through family memory, he may know with a greater intimacy than is ever granted to most of us, Michael Ignatieff, on a visit to Montreal from his home in England, ponders Paul and Natasha and the life that was theirs in the new country a world away from the old.

"How did my grandparents and their children understand what was asked of them when they came to Canada in 1928 compared to what is asked and required of a Haitian arriving in Montreal in the 1980s?" he wonders aloud. "What has changed here? What are you allowed to assert of yourself that you weren't allowed to assert of yourself then?"[4]

The question is cast with an historian's eye, but an historian whose academic training has not robbed him of his sense of the blood and guts of history: people are central; they shape events and are in turn shaped by them. If journalism is the unconsidered reporting of raw history in the form of "facts," and if history is the considered ordering of "facts" into perceived truths, then Michael Ignatieff culls his perceptions from somewhere in the middle ground—after the passions have receded but before the dust has settled.

"I have some sense of a generational change here, that earlier waves of immigration understood integration here as 'We will learn the language, we will learn the values, we will learn the culture'—and some of that had a semi-sacramental importance. My father could always tell you what it was like to stand in line in 1935 at City Hall in Toronto as a young university undergraduate and take the Canadian oath of citizenship: he had a feeling of a tremendously important rite of passage which left him incredibly patriotic as a Canadian to the end.

"I think some of it had to do with destitution. They had nothing when they came and they thought: We're not in a position to dictate the terms here, we're coming to a new, young country and we'll take what we can get. And if that meant being called a Bohunk and all the kinds of Slavic abuse [popular] in the twenties and thirties, well, so be it. They had the sense of this being a porous society, a society that wasn't defining the contract of integration in very demanding ways."[5]

And yet, that contract of integration, while not demanding, had also established parameters of restriction aimed at defining the look of the society that immigration would create.

The Canada the Ignatieffs came to was one in transition. The country, with a population of just over 10 million, had emerged from the First World War bloodied but with a greater sense of itself. No longer content to be merely an adjunct to the British Empire, it began seeking ways to enlarge the colonial envelope, a process legitimized by the 1926 Balfour Declaration, which recognized "Britain and the dominions as equals in a Commonwealth partnership."[6] It was the initiation in Canada of a slow process of decolonization.

Under the guidance of Mackenzie King in particular, Canada's acquiescence to British wishes was no longer automatic, the rush to arms to serve British interests no longer enthusiastic. The urge to greater independence culminated in the 1931 Statute of Westminister, which gave Canada full control over its foreign and domestic policy.

It was, on the whole, a country protective of its racial and cultural exclusivity. The native population was contained on reserves, the small black communities effectively isolated from mainstream life, and entry to Canada by people deemed undesirable on racial and ethnic grounds was severely restricted. American whites were encouraged, American blacks not. Landing fees of $25 or

$50 were charged to all—except for Asians, who were levied $200. In 1923, this requirement was dropped—again except for Asians, who were now required to pay a "head tax" of $250, a measure aimed exclusively at reducing their numbers.

Nor did East Indians, fellow loyalists to the British crown, find favour. One of the more disgraceful incidents in Canadian history began on May 23, 1914, three months before the start of the war that would lead, among other consequences, to the overthrow of the Romanov dynasty in Russia and the uprooting of the Ignatieff family.

On that day, a freighter named the *Komagata Maru* dropped anchor off Vancouver. On board were 376 passengers, all from the Far East, many bearing the Sikh ceremonial name of Singh. The ship was quarantined, sealed off by armed guards, only an official government party allowed onboard or off. Official resistance to their admission to Canada centred on the existence of illness among the would-be migrants: twenty-two would be allowed to land, the others would have to sail on.

In the ensuing stalemate, Immigration officials would not even let garbage off the ship. Food and water began running out. Many more passengers fell ill. One died.

Then, in a move rigid with bureaucratic thinking, it was decided that the fate of the remaining 354 would hinge on a test case of one of their number. A young Sikh farmer was taken to court, quickly ruled inadmissible. (Only a miracle could have led to a different conclusion.) Deportation orders were issued, and, on July 23, 1914, precisely two months after first dropping anchor, the *Komagata Maru* steamed away from Canadian shores.

As Glenda Simms, president of the Canadian Advisory Council on the Status of Women, has written, "This incident is cited in most discussions on state racism in

Canada and serves as a reminder of the many past actions in which the country takes no pride."[7]

But it must be borne in mind that Canadian suspicion of foreigners was not only, or purely, racial in character. The country was often fine in its discriminations. As the historian Ramsay Cook points out,[8] southern Italians, for instance, were viewed as irretrievably corrupt and so, unlike their northern brethren, were not welcome either.

In *None is Too Many*, the chilling study of the effect of Canada's racial policies on the Jews of Europe, Irving Abella and Harold Troper write: "If Canada, unlike the United States, never legislated quotas against particular groups, Canada's government still enforced a restrictive immigration policy with unabashed racial and ethnic priorities. With public support, it knew what ethnic and racial groups it wanted and how to keep out those it did not.... [T]hose groups that did not fit the national vision—especially Jews, Asians and blacks—were ever more often relegated by Canadian officials to the bottom of the list of those preferred."[9]

On the whole, then, immigration at the beginning of the century was restricted to those who, at the end of the century, would be euphemistically referred to by some as "traditional" immigrants, i.e. white and Christian. It was immigration policy defined by a sense of superiority based on race, ethnicity and class-consciousness—which evokes the persistent riddle of why a colonial people so readily adopts the worst traits of the colonial master.

Even acceptance into Canada, though, did not guarantee fair treatment. As the late Ken Adachi points out in *The Enemy that Never Was*,[10] naturalized citizens of Japanese origin and their Canadian-born children were routinely denied basic citizenship rights—the right to vote, the right to exercise certain professions such as law and pharmacy—but were not exempt from taxation or conscription. The distrust and fear of the "yellow peril" (a phrase coined by, of all people, Kaiser Wilhelm II) led to discriminations grand and petty: the 1907 riot in Vancouver, when the Japanese district of "Little Tokyo" was attacked by a mob out for blood; a policy throughout the twenties of reducing the number of fishing licences held by fishermen of Japanese descent, and even denying them the use of gas-powered boats; restrictions in theatres on where they could sit, in swimming pools on when they could swim—all of which culminated, of course, in the forced evacuations, internments and confiscations following the Japanese attack on Pearl Harbor in December 1941.

It is worth remembering, too, that despite the political successes of Sir Wilfrid Laurier, the mass of French Canadians lived with the knowledge that, in the companies they worked for, they would always be the clerks and never the president, and advancement to head clerk required a measure of subservience and proficiency in a language not their own.

This, then, was one aspect of the country to which the Ignatieff family came in 1928, a country of easy social integration, but only for those permissible under the unwritten racial and ethnic policies of the time. As people searching for a haven, for a life to replace the one they had lost, they could not be expected to have been concerned with the easy and ingrained injustices that did not directly affect them. As with all refugees, of far greater concern would have been the battle to secure a future, at a time when the country was sliding into depression. For the moment, it was survival that mattered; the questions of public policy that would concern the sons in later years were an intellectual luxury ill afforded.

It would take decades, and the tragedies of another world war, before Canada would begin to grow out of its anaemic ethical adolescence and challenge itself to engage the complexities of a world in which the certainties and prejudices of empire had been forever shattered.

What kind of government ruled Canada in the prosperous post-war years? To make a simple distinction, two different ethics drive government action. Most legislation follows the developing shape of society; it plays a game of legislative catch-up. If hogs were once legally banned from running along the streets of Toronto, it was because they were doing just that—and causing what one imagines to be a fair amount of malodorous chaos. The resulting legislation was an attempt to address a widely perceived social problem; it was based on a perception of consensus, and enjoyed legitimacy by offering a solution to citizens' anxieties. Legislatures, then, for the most part, follow in the choppy wake of society. Laws in a democratic society are engendered by event.

But activist governments, motivated by a vision not just of what society is but what it should be, are not content just to follow. They will seek, as much as possible, to engage a predetermined ideological agenda, establishing social and legislative programs designed to nudge (or shove) society in directions they deem laudable. It is, to a certain extent, a Platonic approach to government, the construction of myth and structure aimed at the attainment of a reasonable Good. Such a government, philosophically opposed to, say, capital punishment, would initiate a program of persuasion to entice a populace philosophically committed to the death sentence away from it. Sometimes it works, sometimes it does not. Unless opposition is vigorous, though, the activist government will proceed with its agenda, leaving the game of catch-up to the people.

How much to follow, how much to lead? It is the inevitable tension of democratic government. Each approach has its advantages and its disadvantages.

A government that simply follows the wishes of the electorate may appear more democratic, but it also inevitably betrays a basic notion of democracy: if legislative decisions are to be made on the basis of consensus through referendum or poll, then debate, elections and parliaments become pointless. Better to establish a civil service structure responsible for implementing the wishes of the majority as expressed through public opinion survey: the tyranny, then, of the majority.

An activist government, one that defines leadership in terms of (to use a military metaphor) "taking the point," also runs risks. It can lead only so long as the people are willing to follow. Failure to engage the abilities or inclinations of the society will necessarily lead to resentment, resistance, loss of legitimacy—to, with perseverance, the tyranny of a minority. A government outdistances its electorate at its own peril.

Most governments attempt to mediate a line between the two approaches, a line that meanders along the graphs of its popularity.

The choice of the kind of government best suited to a country at any given time in its history is determined by the temper of the people it is meant to serve. A people confident of itself and its future may be eager to be mobilized by visionary leadership, may be keen on the idea of being shown how to be better than it ever thought it could be.

In the 1960s, Canada became this kind of country. The land that had, early in the century, defined itself largely through notions of race was not immune to the powerful liberal ethic that the decade brought to North America.

Canadians, like Americans, had been touched by the wave of inspiration unleashed by John and Robert Kennedy. They too had been inspired by Martin Luther King and had witnessed the frequently violent struggle for civil rights in the United States. They had made known their opposition to the war in Vietnam. And, at home, Quebec dramatically remade itself, almost willing into existence a new and vibrant society from a somnolent rural and religious past.

Out of such ferment, towards the end of the decade, emerged the vitality and apparent activism of Pierre Elliott Trudeau, the man who would remake Canada, a country prepared to follow him out of its traditional staidness into a more exciting version of itself. Trudeau, then, was seen by the Canadian public to be the embodiment of a stylish Vision of the Good.

But an activist Vision of the Good, as already pointed out, rarely suffices on its own. For intellectual belief to be translated into public policy, it must encounter either a certain measure of public support based on ethical belief (such as in the abolition of the death penalty nationally or the establishment in Quebec of legal linguistic parameters, each of which is seen by its supporters as serving a greater good), or it must respond to the narrower demands of partisan political necessity. When these conditions coincide, the government enjoys what is known somewhat inelegantly as "a win-win situation."

Expectations of Trudeau were great. He would renew the country, he would unite it. He would gild us all with the sheen of his personality. The reality could never fit the fantasy. Big ideas came to Ottawa, ideas that prompted a snowstorm of studies and, by most accounting, the barest sprinkling of results. By the third year of his first prime ministerial mandate, the rose was wilting: Trudeaumania was transforming itself into

Trudeauphobia, and concerns about the next campaign, the next mandate, began to make themselves felt. In 1971, with his government sliding steadily into unpopularity (thanks in large part to a policy of bilingualism that had been badly explained and insensitively implemented), Pierre Trudeau initiated a federal policy that would change the face of the nation forever, the official policy of multiculturalism.

> *3. (1) It is hereby declared to be the policy of the Government of Canada to (a) recognize and promote the understanding that multiculturalism reflects the cultural and racial diversity of Canadian society and acknowledges the freedom of all members of Canadian society to preserve, enhance and share their cultural heritage.*
>
> Canadian Multiculturalism Act

Retrospect does not always offer clarity: separating the social necessity from the political can be difficult, if not impossible. Politicians, in interview or in memoir, will always offer the most selfless of justifications—while their opponents will seek to highlight the selfish. It is curious, then, that while vigorously defending bilingualism in his memoirs, Pierre Trudeau never mentions multiculturalism. One cannot help wondering whether this omission can be taken as a measure of his intellectual commitment to the policy.

The view of journalist Richard Gwyn is uncompromising. "Trudeau's imperative, post-1972," he writes, "changed from doing what was right, rationally, to doing what was advantageous politically. So Trudeau had been criticized for ignoring the Queen; in 1973, the Queen came to Canada twice, a history-making precedent, with Trudeau at her side every step of the royal progress. So he had been accused of sloughing off the ethnics; up sprang a trebled multiculturalism program that functioned as a slush fund to buy ethnic votes."[11]

It reads like an indictment, multiculturalism boosted into the limelight not as a progressive social policy but as an opportunistic political one, not so much an answer to necessary social accommodation as a response to pressing political concern. If the emphasis on federal bilingualism had seemed to favour francophone Quebec at the expense of the rest of the country, enhanced multiculturalism could be served up as a way of equalizing the political balance sheet. The activist elected in 1968 became, four years later, the opportunist fighting for his political life.

Former Quebec premier René Lévesque was frankly dismissive of the multicultural game. "Multiculturalism, really, is folklore," he once said. "It is a 'red herring.' The notion was devised to obscure 'the Quebec business,' to give an impression that we are *all* ethnics and do not have to worry about special status for Québec."[12]

This view is shared by the political scientist Christian Dufour, who, in his book *Le Défi québécois*, offers two reasons for the advent of multiculturalism: "It was a matter of responding to the expectations of immigrants who arrived in Ontario after the second world war and whose assimilation had not been completed. But it was also a way of refusing to recognize the bicultural nature of the country and the political consequences of Québécois specificity. Multiculturalism, in principle, reduces the Québécois fact to an ethnic phenomenon."[13]

"A slush fund to buy ethnic votes"; reducing Québec distinctiveness to "an ethnic phenomenon": immigrants, naturalized citizens, "ethnic" Canadians offered a hyphen (and government funds) in exchange for allowing themselves to be used as pawns in the old Canadian tug-of-war between anglophones and francophones. It is a sad and dispiriting view of a policy that, on the face of it, seems suffused with humanism. It is also a view that, in the atmosphere of suspicion that envelops the tug-of-war, has the ring of truth.

But even a program aimed primarily at manipulation may benefit from a certain measure of heart and sincerity.

The Act for the Preservation and Enhancement of Multiculturalism in Canada, better known by its short title, the Canadian Multiculturalism Act, is composed of phrases that bring to mind the Trinidadian expression "sweet talk." It is a document that, through the repetition of gentle and well-meaning generalizations, seeks to seduce.

The act recognizes "the existence of communities whose members share a common origin and their historic contribution to Canadian society" and promises to "enhance their development"; it aims to "promote the understanding and creativity that arise from the interaction between individuals and communities of different origins" and commits the federal government to the promotion of "policies and practices that enhance the understanding of and respect for the diversity of the members of Canadian society." It talks about being "sensitive and responsive to the multicultural reality of Canada."

Recognition, appreciation, understanding; sensitive, responsive, respectful; promote, foster, preserve: these words and others like them occur time and again in the Multiculturalism Act, repeated amidst the thicket of legalistic phrasing like the mantras of goodwill and brotherhood employed by religious cults.

Beyond this, the act goes from the general to the concrete by authorizing the minister responsible to "take such measures as the Minister considers appropriate to...(a) encourage and assist individuals, organizations and institutions to project the multicultural reality of Canada in their activities in Canada and abroad;...(c) encourage and promote exchanges and cooperation among the diverse communities of Canada;...(e) encourage the preservation, enhancement, sharing and evolving expression of the multicultural heritage of Canada;...(h) provide support to individuals, groups or organizations for the purpose of preserving, enhancing and promoting multiculturalism in Canada."

One feels like a bit of an ingrate in admitting that these words evoke less a sigh of reassurance than a shudder of suspicion. Questioning such sentiments is like doubting professions of motherly love: there is something slightly disreputable about it. And yet it is impossible to avoid a whiff of formaldehyde, a hint of the sterility of museum display cases. Impossible to ignore the image of colourful butterflies pinned to black velvet by careful and loving hands all for the greater glory of...the butterflies?

The Multiculturalism Act is in many ways a statement of activism. It is a vision of government not content to let things be, determined to play a direct role in shaping not only the evolution of Canadian—mainly *English*-Canadian—society but the evolution of individuals within that society as well. As a political statement it is disarming, as a philosophical statement almost naïve with generosity. Attractive sentiments liberally dispensed—but where, in the end, do they lead?

The act, activist in spirit, magnanimous in accommodation, curiously excludes any ultimate vision of the kind of society it wishes to create. It never addresses the question of the nature of a multicultural society, what such a society is and—beyond a kind of vague notion of respect for human differences—what it means for the nation at large and the individuals who compose it. Definitions and implications are conspicuously absent, and this may be indicative of the political sentiments that prompted the adoption of the act in the first place. Even years later, the act—a cornerstone of bipartisan, federal social policy—shows signs of a certain haste. In its lack of long-term consideration, in its promise of action with no discussion of consequence, one can discern the opportunism that underlay it all. One senses the political hand, eager for an instrument to attract "ethnic" votes, urging along the drafting—and damn the consequences.

In its rush, the act appears to indulge in several unexamined assumptions: that people, coming here from elsewhere, wish to remain what they have been; that personalities and ways of doing things, ways of looking at the world, can be frozen in time; that Canadian cultural influences pale before the exoticism of the foreign. It views newcomers as exotics, and pretends that this is both proper and sufficient.

Nor does the act address the question of limits: how far do we go as a country in encouraging and promoting cultural difference? How far is far enough, how far too far? Is there a point at which diversity begins to threaten social cohesion? The document is striking in its lack of any mention of unity or oneness of vision. Its provisions seem aimed instead at encouraging division, at ensuring that the various ethnic groups whose interests it espouses discover no compelling reason to blur the distinctions among them.

A cynic might be justified in saying that this is nothing more than a cleverly disguised blueprint for a policy of "keep divided and therefore conquered," a policy that seeks merely to keep a diverse populace amenable to political manipulation.

The Canadian Multiculturalism Act is in many senses an ill-considered document, focused so squarely on today that it ignores tomorrow. And its very short-sightedness might account for the consequences it has brought about—for individuals, families, communities and the country as a whole.

It was a policy initiated by an activist government anxious about its future. The populace was willing to follow at the time—a happy conjunction of purpose for the Trudeau government—but, if the polls are correct, this may no longer be so twenty years later. The temper of the country has altered, its circumstances changed. The same people who, in the sixties, were eager for leadership now seek a certain paternalism. Demoralized, enervated by social and economic adversity, they have turned resentful. They have grown conservative and self-protective, desirous not of the brave new world but of the safe old one. Times have changed, and a good idea then may not be a good idea now—not only because the country is no longer what it once was but also because the policy itself has, in the eyes of many, been frittered away into disillusionment and discredit.

Reality has a way of battering philosophy: it is reality's way of saying a new philosophy must be found. It may be time for the cow of multiculturalism to be stripped of its holiness.

Four

Losing the Centre

There is no way to make people like change. You can only make them feel less threatened by it.

Frederick Hayes
Fortune Magazine
1969

Comparing the Canada of 1928, to which his grandparents came, with the Canada of 1994, to which so many come, Michael Ignatieff wonders what has changed.

The answer, in short, is everything. As a society, we have gone from one defined by colonialism through reference to the British crown to one seeking definition through references to self; from a society of almost uniform colour to one that is multi-hued; from a society that was of almost uniform religion to one that is multi-faithed. The traditional notions of Canada, then, representing the centre of the nation's being, are being challenged, even effaced, by the need for transition—a need created, to a large degree, by multiculturalism.

It is a transition that has grown uneasy with the years.

The Importance of Millinery

The defining issue is, on the face of it, absurd, revolving as it does around the question of if and when to cover our heads, and with what. The appropriateness of headgear has become a burning issue in Canada at the end of the twentieth century. It is tempting to say that it is a happy country indeed that can be aroused over elements of millinery, but insecurities will sometimes manifest themselves in absurd ways.

On November 11, 1993, five Sikh veterans who had participated in Remembrance Day ceremonies were refused admittance to the main hall of the Newton branch of the Royal Canadian Legion in the Vancouver suburb of Surrey. Branch by-laws prohibited the wearing of headgear as a sign of respect for fallen comrades. Since the Sikhs would not remove their turbans, they were invited to "go into a separate room by themselves to drink coffee."[1] *The Globe and Mail* report quoted at least one Legion member angered by the treatment afforded the Sikhs—but television news reports in the following days also offered the ugly sight of angry members calling on the Sikhs to go back where they came from.

Reaction was swift and uncompromising. National Legion headquarters, the Dominion Command, formally apologized to the Sikhs and condemned their treatment, as did the provincial minister for Women's Equality, who had attended the ceremonies, and the British Columbia Federation of Labour.

The branch, however, would not be swayed. Branch president Frank Underwood told the *Globe*: "I was very proud to see these [Sikh] guys march, I was proud to see them do their thing in the war, but regulations and rules are regulations and rules."[2] He was not alone in his sentiments.

Other branches took the same stand as the issue

caught fire. In Jasper, Alberta, one Sikh was refused entrance to the Legion hall where his wife's staff Christmas party was being held, while in Red Deer, the secretary of the Alberta Liberal Party, a turbanned Sikh, was loudly insulted as he walked through the Legion hall on the way to a political fund-raising event. In Cornwall, Ontario, a split opened up in the Legion membership following a statement by the branch president to a local newspaper: "When in Rome, you do as the Romans. If they [Sikh veterans] feel they have to wear their turbans, then let them go back to their country and do what they want to do."[3] (It never seems to have occurred to the president, a man with the traditional Canadian name of Angelo Lebano, that Canada may be the country of the the Sikh veterans as much as it is his.)

Fear radicalizes. On May 31, 1994, at the Legion's national convention in Calgary, delegates voted overwhelmingly against a proposal to permit religious headgear of any kind into their halls. One delegate said, "I honestly feel that everybody in Canada is getting sick and tired of this human rights [issue]. Where are our human rights? We fought for this country." Another said, "I say to hell with 'em—take them on because they've been taking us on."[4] These are words of anger and of fear, the words of people caught in the slipstream of history.

Three days later, three days before the fiftieth anniversary of the Normandy invasion and on the very day that Queen Elizabeth II was dedicating a new Canadian war monument near Buckingham Palace, *The Globe and Mail* reported on its front page that many Legion halls in Alberta that ban turbans and yarmulkes permit the wearing of cowboy hats during events such as the Calgary Stampede: "The leaders said the hats are allowed because they reflect a pride of members in the the western tradition." As well, an employee at a British Columbia branch admitted that members and guests wearing baseball hats were regularly served, unchallenged. It wasn't worth the trouble, he said, undaunted by the hypocrisy.

As spectacle the controversy was sad, but its saddest aspect is the evident blindness to the larger historical context that binds these people together, a context that resurges in moments such as this one:

> CASSINO, Italy—British and Commonwealth veterans of the battle of Monte Cassino gathered yesterday to pay tribute to fallen comrades on the 50th anniversary of one of the bloodiest campaigns of the Second World War...
>
> Many saluted and others shed tears as buglers sounded *The Last Post* and three volleys of gunfire rang out, breaking the silence among the rows of low white gravestones that mark where 4,265 British and Commonwealth soldiers lie.
>
> [T]he service...brought together survivors from Britain, New Zealand, South Africa, India, Canada and other Commonwealth countries.[5]

Were there Sikhs, turbanned and bemedalled, among the old soldiers? And were the memories consequently any less striking, was the comradeship any less intense, the tribute to fallen comrades any less sincere?

Veterans are proud people, and rightfully so. Though many of them are physically diminished by age, their handshakes tend to be firm, their gazes frank. But they are also people prey to the insecurities of change. It is important to realize that the membership of the Newton branch is racially varied, and this has never been in question. It is also important to remember that it is not "the veterans" who have taken a stand against turbans, who have made hurtful comments, but *some* veterans in *some* Legion halls. The historical accomplishments of the many must not be attenuated by the publicized foolishness of the few.

Meanwhile, on another front, an old fight long presumed over continued over turbans in the RCMP as a group of retired officers, offended by the RCMP commissioner's 1990 decision to allow the wearing of turbans in the force, asked the federal court to reverse the policy. They were backed up by a 210,000-name petition and 9,000 letters supporting their contention that "the change undermines the non-religious nature of the force."[6] Canadians, the plaintiffs' lawyer said, "have a constitutional right to a secular state free of religious symbols."

It is a compelling, and profoundly flawed, argument—or, at least, an argument which, if judged to have merit, would necessitate a slew of changes to traditional Canadian symbols. If the ideals of a secular state would forbid turbans in the RCMP, so must they also forbid the use of the Bible in court for swearing to tell the truth; so must they forbid the mention of the word God in the swearing in of cabinet ministers and new citizens. All forms of prayer must be banished from the federal Parliament and provincial legislatures, as must be turbans from Parliament and courtrooms—which would create an active discrimination by effecively barring Canadians of the Sikh religion from the political and judicial life of the nation. And, as a lawyer representing the Alberta Civil Liberties Association pointed out, Canada's "coat-of-arms includes the Union Jack—which is made up of three religious crosses." The strict preservation of one tradition, then, must logically lead to the dismantling of many others—a pyrrhic victory at best.

It is curious that the former officers would be so exercised by a length of wound cloth: the RCMP appears too robust an organization to have its very essence threatened by a turban or two or three among the stetsons. And if the idea behind the challenge is to preserve tradition, to ensure that all Mounties of tomorrow look precisely like all Mounties of yesterday, should not the force return to patrolling the highways and byways of the land as tradition dictates—dressed in scarlet and mounted on horseback?

The preservation of traditions is important, within reason. Tradition—the comfort of continuity, the picket-fence of privilege—is not immutable. Yesterday's ways must adapt to today's changed circumstances. The RCMP has, through the decades, adapted admirably to changing times: automobiles, walkie-talkies, police caps, etc. Adaptability seems, however, to freeze before this bizarre Canadian obsession with headgear.

It is an obsession that has entered even the courts.

On November 29, 1993, in the Montreal suburb of Longueuil, municipal court Judge Richard Alary expelled a Muslim woman for wearing a hijab—a traditional head scarf—in his courtroom. In the view of the judge, court rules banning headgear took precedence over religious freedom as enshrined in the Canadian Charter of Rights and Freedoms. It was explained that the hijab, like the Sikh turban, is more than simply a hat; it is an intimate part of religious identity; it is, for the believer, vital. The explanation made no difference.

Even after the president of the Quebec Municipal Judges Conference, Judge Raymond Lavoie, announced that "no rule exists that prevents Muslims—or people of any faith—from wearing a religious headdress in court,"[7] the woman, Ouafa Mousselyne, born in Morocco, found herself subjected to intense questioning at a disciplinary hearing into the judge's conduct ordered by Justice Minister Gil Rémillard. According to a report in the

Montreal *Gazette*, Judge Alary's lawyer, Gabriel Lapointe, "grilled Mousselyne about her marriage, divorce, relationship with another man, her travels, work history, the frequency with which she prays every day and the number of times she visits a mosque every week."[8] Just as rape victims could once be grilled on their sexual history, so this woman was being grilled on her religious history in an attempt to establish the depth of her religious commitment: it is like saying that if you do not attend church every Sunday you are not a real Christian. Lapointe offered the opinion "that Mousselyne may have worn the hijab as a legal tactic—not out of religious conviction." The point is remarkably pointless. Not only does it ignore the absence of rules on headgear but, frankly speaking, is there a defence lawyer who would not pour his client, no matter how unkempt in everyday life, into an ill-fitting suit for a court date? Appearance is a legal tactic, and Mousselyne, like all defendants, was entitled to it. None of this had any bearing on the judge's conduct.

Some months later, Judge Alary, clearly a man of conviction and courage, gave a speech to the Centre Maghrébien de Recherche et d'Information de Montréal in which he presented a defence of himself and his actions. "If I were not a believer of the Catholic faith," he asserted, "I would probably be a Muslim. Not only have I always been fascinated by Islam, but I've also always greatly admired and respected the Muslims for their attachment to their religion."[9] He spoke of that fascination in both intellectual and emotional terms and denied having expelled Mrs. Mousselyne because of her religion. He admitted to wondering about the motive for the scarf worn by Mrs. Mousselyne and about its appropriateness as regards the rules of decorum (no unbuttoned or sleeveless shirts or blouses; no shorts, bathing suits, hats, headdresses, sunglasses, gum, tobacco or food). With evident passion, he also disassociated himself from attempts to portray him as a hero courageous enough "to face the Muslims."

One cannot doubt the good judge's assertion of admiration for Islam and its practitioners; he is clearly distressed by motives of intolerance ascribed to him. His sincerity must therefore be taken at its word—and yet one cannot, at the same time, escape ironic echoes of "Some of my best friends are (fill in the blank)...."

In Toronto, too, the question of headgear in court arose during the trial of black activist Dudley Laws on Immigration Act charges. As *Globe and Mail* columnist Michael Valpy put it, several men and women in the courtroom were "wearing headgear representing various spiritual and cultural motivations."[10] The judge, Mr. Justice H. C. Whealy, was not happy at the sight and delivered himself of a lengthy statement on proper attire in his courtroom in which he established certain "recognizable boundaries" such as: male heads must remain uncovered; female headgear "must not interfere with other members of the public or be flamboyant"; "bizarre and intrusive attire, something that immediately draws attention from the proceedings" is unwelcome. He also banned "signs, pennants, other intrusive indicia." These are reasonable guidelines intended to assure a certain decorum—"demeanour, solemnity and dignity"—vital to the efficient functioning of the courtroom.

But then the judge entered a more unsettling realm:

> Some head coverings, by their shape, colour and design, are obviously and easily recognizable as signalling to the eye an adherent of a well-established and recognizable race, culture, national or religious community, one of those

> communities [which are] clearly within the purview of the Charter....
>
> There are, as well, many self-proclaimed and unrecognized forms of religion or cults claiming to be religious which have occurred not only this year, but throughout history. They come and go.
>
> Often to attract new attention and new adherents, bizarre, intrusive or simply impolite attire is worn.
>
> These religions may exist and may have limited Charter protection, but the Charter does not guarantee some right to enter and remain in a courtroom where the result is disruptive. A public trial does not include offensive or intrusive costumes.
>
> It is for the judge to decide if the intrusion is derogatory to the proper process of the court. It is a question of judgment.

He set himself up, in other words, as judge not just of the case before him—a job for which he was undoubtedly qualified—but of the validity of the religious expression entering his courtroom, of which religion or cults would come and go. It is a judgment likely to be based on notions of "demeanour, solemnity and dignity" established in the old Canada and therefore challenged by aspects of the new: one culture's flamboyance is another culture's norm. In another courtroom, in another land, certain headgear or clothing would be simply part of the scenery. In the traditional Canadian context, however, they are "intrusive" and likely to draw attention from the proceedings.

Mr. Justice Whealy's statement, then, is the old Canada establishing the limits of its tolerance within the context of the courtroom. It is, from a philosophical point of view, not unlike the veterans' reaction to turbans in the Legion hall, or RCMP officers' reactions to turbans in the force: a certain vision of what constitutes decorum—an attitude of respect—hurtles into another vision of the same thing. Mr. Justice Whealy is trying to control his turf in the same way that the veterans are trying to control theirs, each trying with varying degrees of eloquence to define the challenged centre.

Headgear is not the only issue to have focused fears over the loss of the old Canada. Other manifestations of traditional Canada, particularly the cultural aspects of religion, have also come under revision.

Christmas concerts in schools, for example, are now distinguished by the fact that they have had the Christianity removed from them in order to spare the feelings of non-Christians. Christmas, as a result, is reduced, as Michael Valpy put it, "to artistically bad commercial songs extolling the materialism around Santa Claus. The great music of Christmas, the universal human meaning of Christmas, is all eliminated."[11] As Christmas 1993 approached, even an Ontario civil servant in the town of Sudbury sought to ensure inoffensiveness by issuing a memo directing that decorations in public places "conform to a seasonal theme rather than Christmas iconography," the justification being that the government "is not in the position of promoting one religion over others, and in respect of our multicultural society, we should show sensitivity."[12] The directive became public—and was quickly cancelled.

This does not mean there must be no change—but change does not have to be exclusive. A small example: In the winter of 1993, the Warden Woods Shopping Centre in the Toronto suburb of Scarborough, in order "to reflect the multicultural nature of Canada,"[13] as the Canadian Press report put it, instigated a theme called "Santas from Around the World." The costumes were traditional red, the beards traditional white—but some of the faces behind the beards were less than traditional: Santa was sometimes black, sometimes Asian, and he sometimes he spoke with a Trinidadian or Pakistani accent. One (white) Santa worried that "the campaign might offend some people," but as a black Santa pointed out, "Santa Claus is a universal figure." Just as the Pope does not have to be Italian, so Santa Claus does not have to be white—or fat, for that matter.

There are two ways in which the question of Santa's colour could have been addressed: 1) ban Santa Claus or 2) do precisely what the mall did. Is it a reason for hope or for despair that a government bureaucrat chose to be exclusive, while a shopping mall chose to be inclusive?

Another example of truly sensitive change occurred early in 1994 when the House of Commons, without opposition, voted to change the wording of the prayer with which it had begun its business every morning for one hundred and six years. The old prayer, as majestic as it was archaic, sought blessings for the entire royal family in terms and language as ornately Christian as it is possible to be. To general media applause—the Montreal *Gazette* stated that "Canada is a country of religious diversity, where no one religion should be seen as synonymous with the state"[14]; the *Globe and Mail* admitted that, "Yes, it was wrong, in a time of growing religious and cultural diversity, for the daily prayer in the House of Commons to include references to 'Jesus Christ our Lord.' Yes, the Commons was right to compose a new, more ecumenical prayer."[15]—its musty beauty was replaced with a shorter, less exalted but certainly more inclusive declaration. It was a rare example of leadership—the tug of tradition, the acceptance of changed times—and a recognition of the many "minority" members of the House, where, openly at least, the wearing of turbans is not an issue.

But consider the words of reticent Reform MP Myron Thompson when asked about the right of non-Christian MPs to have a prayer reflective of their beliefs: "I'm sure that if I went to *their* country and went into *their* House of Commons that they wouldn't change their prayers to suit my needs."[16] Is *their* country not Canada? Is *their* House of Commons not in Ottawa? Explicit in Mr. Thompson's objection, stated to reporters but unregistered in the vote, was his worry over the disappearance of the old Canada: "Canada shouldn't change and adapt and get away from the founding principles and values that this country was built on, and that was the Christian faith." A dinosaur, one might be tempted to say, but how terrifying it must be—for Mr. Thompson, for the recalcitrant veterans, for the retired RCMP officers—to see the world in which they grew up change so dramatically before their eyes.

Christmas iconography, Christian prayers: it is difficult to imagine the grounds for offence. The idea of banning Christmas trees and angels from office lobbies, of preventing children from staging a nativity scene, strikes me as outrageous and absurd as the banning of turbans in Legion halls and the RCMP. The exclusion of some beliefs, or their manifestations, does not make for the inclusion of others. Religious belief so fragile as to be threatened by the mere sight of Christian iconography is hardly belief at all.

The most religiously insistent people I have ever known were my grandmothers.

One practised her religion assiduously, with frequent trips to the Hindu temple. Her beliefs were her own. She tried to foist them on no one.

My other grandmother was more of a missionary with her beliefs. She sought constantly to seduce others into her frequent religious ceremonies, and it may have been a source of some private pain to her that she succeeded so rarely. It was a change beyond her—and our—control, a change wrought by history and success: a family that had laboured on the land had gone, in one generation, to professional offices—lawyers, doctors, successful businessmen—and from religious ideas to university ideas, the world opening up from travel mandated by poverty to travel sought for pleasure. The comfort she had found in religion was gained by her children in more worldly ways—and the pride she took in her offsprings' achievements must have been mingled with a certain fear of the dramatic changes brought by those achievements to her children and her grandchildren.

My primary school in Trinidad was founded by Presbyterian missionaries from Canada. Every school day began with a prayer service, and the highlight of every Christmas was a nativity play in which everyone, Christian and non-Christian, was included (an approach that can be interpreted as either respectful or disrespectful of other religious persuasions). For me as a young boy, it was far better to be with my friends, to be included in their events. And it was in the nearby church one Christmas, with my parents and grandparents in the audience, that this inclusion led to an undistinguished theatrical debut.

As theatrical costumes go, mine was on the simple side: my father's old terrycloth bathrobe striped in muted blues, greys and reds belted around my waist, and a length of egg-yellow cloth, unhemmed and fraying, held draped on my head by my mother's blue bandeau. An outfit, then, that merited the word "ratty," but sufficient to transform a ten-year-old Trinidadian Hindu into Joseph, husband of the Mother of God. My lack of either theatrical ambition or religious belief were of little consequence to my teacher, a man who related the most marvellous tales of Biblical blood-letting at the morning worship.

After almost three decades, little of the play itself remains with me. My teacher's daughter played Mary, his son the Roman guard declaiming the familiar story, the Three Wise Men, the guards and the flock of angels appointed from among the various religions that filled the class. Jesus, a doll, was the only participant without religion, or dark skin; unswaddled and "awake," he was blond-haired, blue-eyed and graced with red lips of suspiciously feminine aspect.

The highlight of the play for me came after the applause when, as we exited the church into a warm tropical night, one of the Roman guards offered me his wooden spear. He would not part with his sword, but that was all right. At home, the Christmas tree was waiting, Santa due in a few days. There was a family gathering to come on Christmas Eve, songs about dashing through the snow on an open sleigh still to be sung.

As we walked to the cars, my grandmother offered her compliments on a job well done. I do not recall my response, but I remember wondering what she really thought, this woman whose belief in the Hindu pantheon was absolute. She never shared her thoughts, and I was not yet of an age to find it remarkable that in her living room, beside a smaller room in which the Hindu gods stood clustered in effigy, were a small, artificial Christmas tree and gifts to be given in honour of a celebration not her own.

It was, on a visceral level, the truest acceptance of life's variety, and an undeniable sign of the firmness of her faith.

The argument often made in favour of considering Canada a Christian country is that over 90 percent of Canadians, when asked, describe themselves as Christian. It is an impressive figure, but it may be less monolithic than it appears: if necessary, I could describe myself (because of my family, because of my background) as Hindu, but this does not mean I believe in or would insist upon Hinduism. In addition, a place such as, say, Northern Ireland is in all likelihood 100 percent Christian—but there Christian Catholics and Christian Protestants spend an inordinate amount of time and ingenuity seeking ways to obliterate each other: their common Christianity is meaningless in the political and economic scheme of things.

Most important, though, is the simple fact that Canada, a country without a state religion, is devoted to the separation of church and state. Basic human principles—injunctions against stealing, killing, etc.—cross all religious lines. To speak of a "Christian" country, then, is to raise the spectre of religious intolerance.

Evidence of this is provided by a disagreement that broke out during the triennial meeting of the Canadian Council of Churches in May 1994.[17] Council president, the Reverend Bruce McLeod, read a sermon that "suggested that Jesus Christ is not the only valid basis for religion.... Mr. McLeod said that although there is only one God, many different faiths have different ways of reaching God. He added that God would not be pleased if all Hindus, for example, were to be converted to Christianity." This vision—a plea for religious tolerance, which Mr. McLeod defended by pointing out that "We live in diversity, and sometimes diversity is hard to live with," proved disturbing to some conservative delegates, who interpreted the words as "a diminution of the role of Jesus Christ in Christianity." One co-signer of a letter of protest said, "We in the Reformed Church do not believe all religions are windows to God," adding that the conversion of all Hindus to Christianity would lead to "rejoicing in heaven."

Homogeneous Canada, a reality only so long as its minorities could be ignored, is no more. It has become increasingly difficult to imagine that Canada is, or ever was, an exclusively "white Christian country." And if it was once a "British" country, in the cultural sense of the word, it remains so only in redoubts of insecurity sliding uneasily into the pages of history.

To assert Canada's essential Britishness is to ignore the culture and history of French Canada. It may therefore be that this diminishment of traditional (English) Canada is not unintentional, that its reduction to almost "ethnic" status is part of a necessary and unstated adjustment in the psychology that has, in the view of Christian Dufour, governed English-French relations since the fall of Quebec to General Wolfe in 1759. Canada is, in Dufour's view, a country "built on the Conquest":

> People are often very surprised that Quebecers say they are still affected by an event that took place over two hundred years ago, while other peoples have already overcome more recent, more devastating defeats. They forget the fundamental difference between defeat and conquest. A conquest is a permanent defeat, an institutionalized defeat....
>
> In accordance with international law of the

> times, England acquired, in principle, limitless power over [the Canadiens]. That is the ultimate catastrophe for a people: being taken over, totally and permanently, by the hereditary enemy. Contrary to the vanquished, the conquered is affected at the heart of his collective identity. He becomes the conqueror's creature, to do with what he may. That the conqueror is magnanimous changes nothing in this reality. On the contrary, it makes the conquest more humiliating because the conquered also has to be grateful.[18]

If the French never lost the mentality of the conquered, the English never lost the mentality of the conqueror. The events before, during and after the Battle of the Plains of Abraham continue to haunt the relationship on which the modern Canadian state is built. It is a subtle argument, one that makes great sense from the viewpoint of Quebec, where history lives, and perhaps less sense from the viewpoint of English Canada, where history is little more than a fading memory of yesterday's breakfast. A failure to appreciate the power of this psychological imbalance, though, is to condemn ourselves to the kind of Sisyphean constitutional wrangling that has bedevilled us for decades.

There are two possible resolutions to this dilemma: 1) the separation of Quebec from the Canadian state, or 2) the enhancement of the conquered hand in hand with the diminishment of the conqueror to a certain notion of parity.

Federalists, recognizing that the full integration of Quebec into Canada required political and psychological accommodation on both sides, chose the second route: the attraction of French Canadians to federalism through a policy of bilingualism, and the psychological disarming of English Canadians through a policy of multiculturalism.

Multiculturalism, in other words, is the instrument by which the historical arrogance of English Canada towards Quebec—an arrogance that is the psychological inheritance of the Conquest—is expunged, parity established by the casting of both Quebec and traditional "British" Canada as large ethnic groups undistinguished except by their historical roles. In this way, Pierre Trudeau may have been more subtle than we—or he—knew.

Let me make it clear that I do not mean to suggest the existence of a grand machiavellian plot, only that a given public policy reverberates through a variety of public problems. Sometimes the reverberation is planned, sometimes it is not. Sometimes it is desirable, sometimes it is not. And always there are consequences, some foreseen, some not. It is vital to realize that multiculturalism has served political ends far beyond its stated intent of enhancing and preserving exotic ethnicities. To understand this is to understand why, at the end of the twentieth century, so many Canadians are aroused over millinery.

The Rise of the Right

Into this uncertainty—or to a certain extent spawned by it—has stepped the political right, a part of the political spectrum which, even in its most activist ideas, more often than not appears driven simply by its fears. Whether addressing the deficit, the cost of the social safety net, immigration, multiculturalism or bilingualism, the right expresses a vision that is a fantasy of a return to the days when every budget spawned a surplus, every man provided for his family, newcomers were mostly white ("traditional" immigrants), minorities knew their place and everybody spoke English.

On a social level, the void created by multiculturalism policy—the sense of drift and powerlessness that grips so many—is fertile soil for those who, like former U.S. president Ronald Reagan and former British prime minister Margaret Thatcher, hunger for a return to the conservative values of yesterday: the values that were definitions of their own power.

The Reform Party and its leader, Preston Manning, are the most organized expression of this uneasiness, and their electoral success is the most visible expression of it. A vote for Reform appears to be at once a vote of protest, against the present, and a vote of retroactive activism, in favour of the past. The *white* past, many would say—despite well-meaning measures to protect itself from racist policy and personnel, the party has been dogged by charges of racism. This is a result partly of the "populism" it preaches ("Come one, come all!") and partly of philosophical policies untempered by experience.

In his political autobiography *The New Canada*, Mr. Manning makes clear his personal abhorrence of racism and repeats frequently his commitment "to distance [the party] from policy proposals and ideas with a potential for racism."[19]

There is no doubt that Preston Manning himself is a fair and honest, if possibly somewhat naïve, man. Nor is there any doubt, however, that fairness and honesty are qualities easily projected through the vague and vetted wording of public pronouncements. Party language policy (French only in Quebec, English only elsewhere) and party immigration policy (the firm rejection of racial criteria) he qualifies as "balanced and positive"[20] and "racially neutral."[21]

The party's stand on multiculturalism is, at first glance, a sensible one: "The Reform Party believes that cultural development and preservation ought to be the responsibility of individuals, groups, and, if necessary in certain cases (for example, in the case of Quebec and Canadian aboriginals), of provincial and local governments. The role of the federal government should be neutral toward culture just as it is toward religion."[22]

Sensible, yes, but only on the face of it. Reform does not propose the abandonment of the Canadian mosaic—they too are courting ethnic votes—but Mr. Manning does manage to slip an entirely new element into the discussion: for the first time, to my knowledge, Canadian natives are presented as one ethnic group among many, which is a neat way of sloughing off historical betrayals in need of expiation and disenfranchisement in need of rectification. There is more here, one suspects, than meets the eye.

The party's Statement of Principles comes, as is to be expected, cast in language meant to seduce: values and principles; dynamic and constructive change; renewal; value and dignity; fundamental justice; foster and protect, encourage and respect (both in reference to free enterprise); freedom of conscience and religion; accountability; the rule of law. They are comforting words, soothing words—and words with an effect not very different from those in the Multiculturalism Act. There is nothing objectionable here, nothing that would, in the vagueness of sentiment, set alarm bells ringing. But a statement of intent is one thing, the drafting of policy quite another.

If certain Reform Party policies, such as its massive, across-the-board cut in federal expenditures as a way of decapitating the deficit, seem simplistic, others are simply contradictory or vague to the point of slipperiness.

Reform, Mr. Manning has often declared, is "a pro-immigration party" but manages nevertheless to advocate a massive reduction in the numbers accepted, from 250,000 to 150,000.[23] In addition, Mr. Manning insists that Canada must continue to accept "the settlement of genuine refugees who find their way to Canada."[24] However, he added in an interview, claimants "would not be entitled to all the provisions of the Charter just because they managed to get a foot on Canadian soil."[25] Asked how a refugee claimant's status would be determined without benefit of a hearing or trial, Mr. Manning said that was still to be worked out, and then let slip the party's true policy, the gist of which "would be to give immigration officers at border points more power to turn back refugee claimants"[26]—which is not unlike dealing with the problem of, say, homelessness by averting your gaze from the homeless.

As befits its "populist" roots, these are policies that smack of armchair politics, of the bore at a party who, exercised by his daily newspaper, not only has the answers to all social ills but can also tell the Expos how to win the World Series and the Leafs how to win the Stanley Cup. He remains unaware only of his own ignorance and his inability to grapple with complexity. Inconsistency of thought, though, is not a quality that deters the rudderless: Ronald Reagan, too, enjoyed a simple-mindedness and a befuddlement capable of stilling a sense of drift.

Even as it performs in Parliament, the Reform Party continues to puzzle. Like the NDP, with which it shares an unbecoming self-righteousness, it seems less a party of government than of opposition. Shadows lurk behind its pronouncements as it continues to be haunted by some of the more wayward tentacles of its roots. Despite the best efforts of Mr. Manning, the party has been unable to distance itself from a perception of racism:

* October 13, 1993: John Beck, Reform candidate in the Ontario riding of York-Centre, resigns at

the party's request following charges of racism based on anti-immigrant statements he had made. He had also offered to "take a reporter on a tour of Toronto to show him evidence of satanic messages."[27]

* October 13, 1993: Herbert Grubel, Reform candidate in the Capilano-Howe Sound riding of British Columbia, declares new immigrants to be a burden on society. Mr. Grubel, an economics professor at Simon Fraser University, had previously published a paper suggesting that "Canadians were opposed to government policy that allowed large number of 'non-traditional immigrants' into the country."[28]

* John Tillman, a Reform Party official in Nova Scotia, writes a gloating letter to a defeated Conservative candidate in which he refers to women's and minority groups as "parasites of society."[29] He also attacks the candidate for "speaking out for women, homosexuals and minorities."

If the Reform Party has succeeded in earning the trust of many, it has done so despite itself.

With all its contradictions, its vagueness, its hints of measured ruthlessness, the Reform Party nevertheless met with impressive success in the 1993 federal election, a sign, one suspects, of the depth of the unease the party has tapped into—an unease engendered in large part by the cultural void created through multiculturalism policy. It has benefited from fear and a sense of drift, and in this way, shares a phenomenon with Reaganism.

Though the most visible manifestation of the political right in Canada, Reform—because it is a party with political aspirations, because it has legitimized a fair share of private lunacy—is neither its most effective nor its most candid representative. That task falls to individuals with less at stake. People like Andrew Coyne of *The Globe and and Mail*'s editorial board, an articulate, charming and intellectually intense thirty-three-year-old. Or *Maclean's* columnist Barbara Amiel, who frequently comes across as a younger, more stylish and equally combative version of Margaret Thatcher. They tend to be gifted and ambitious people who affect a certain urbanity and who frequently claim that final refuge of the intellectual, common sense.

The most complete rendering of the right-wing vision in Canada, however, may be William Gairdner's treatise *The Trouble with Canada.*[30] An immensely popular and controversial book (the hardcover edition enjoyed seven months on the *Globe and Mail* best-seller list), the title alone is revealing: the book is a litany of intellectualized fears.

Like many of the new conservatives, Mr. Gairdner is an elegantly turned-out, eloquent and charming man. His book, written in an accessible voice ("Let us review the sequence of events ...") and packed with graphs and statistics, strikes all the "right" notes. A few examples:

* Homosexuality is one of several (unnamed) "perverse anti-family sexual 'orientations,'"[31] and Ontario's Bill 54 "has the unfortunate effect of giving homosexuality the status of normal behaviour."[32]

* State financial support for single parents is subsidizing "illegitimacy."

* Bilingualism is the "Master Plan for the Francization of Canada."[33]

* Feminism, always "radical," seeks nothing less than "the radical restructuring of society through centralized social engineering of the most insidious kind.... It aims to destroy much that is good in our society, and replace it with something that is not."[34]

* On gender roles, Mr. Gairdner is particularly creative. Homosexuality, he writes, "thrives when male/female role distinctions are discouraged. Cultures that want to guard against the threat of homosexuality must therefore drive a cultural wedge down hard between maleness and femaleness, for it is no simple coincidence that homosexuality is flourishing in a time of feminism. They go together like two sides of a coin."[35] He laments that a blurring of roles has deprived women of "the one sure control they had over men, the one sure method that enabled women to have children, provide for them, protect them, and nurture them *personally* at the same time."[36]

It is a picture then of a society inhabited by men threatened by women into homosexuality, a picture the corollary of which is a society of GI Joes and Barbies, of men who are men and women who are women, where Joe earns the bread and Barbie breeds the babies; a society of hypocrisy in which women manipulate men in order to safely fulfil their biological destiny, and in which homosexuals must once more secrete their "perversions" in the proverbial closet.

Like many who perceive threat all around, Mr. Gairdner tends to see the world in black-and-white terms, good guys and bad guys, cops and robbers, cowboys and Indians. Plots—anti-family, anti-white, anti-English, anti-male—abound.

The Trouble with Canada is not a work of great subtlety in either style or content, but it is a book permeated with provocation and alarm, drawing explicitly on resentment born of the uncertainty of drift. Even though dressed up in intellectual finery, these remain simple fears, but fears that are not to be dismissed or taken lightly. The flakiness of the conclusions does not nullify the legitimacy of the fears, for one senses the insecurity of someone challenged to his core. "At present," Mr. Gairdner writes, "Canada is in the process of endangering its very existence as a nation at the hands of successive governments that have wilfully undermined our core values and traditions."[37]

On the question of the ethnic composition of the country—intimately linked with immigration and multiculturalism—Mr. Gairdner is explicit in preferring immigrants who "share our moral, legal, cultural and racial heritage."[38] He expresses surprise that the point system for selecting immigrants currently in use has no criteria for culture, race or religion[39] and bemoans the fact that so few British citizens—who, he assumes, share his listed notions of heritage—now emigrate to Canada.

However, in view of the "and" at the end of the list, a young man of, say, East Indian descent born, raised and educated in England, fully sharing in the moral, legal and cultural heritage of the British Isles, would be excluded on racial grounds—yet someone sharing in the legal, cultural and racial heritage, but silently disdainful of its moral aspects, would not be: the skin is visible; moral belief is not. His presentation of a graph demonstrating the dramatic percentage decline of Canadians who say they are of "British extraction" ends in the following way: "It merely reflects present trends, which may alter and...it could be worse. Although I have softened the trend somewhat to avoid the charge of alarmism, it still looks alarming to me!"[40]

Like Preston Manning's "policy" on refugees, Mr. Gairdner's prescription for future immigration is slippery. Without ever saying so, perhaps even without realizing it, he proposes an immigration policy of fundamentally racial character—and the application of epithets such as "traditional" and "non-traditional" to immigration does nothing to hide the fact. If "traditional" does not denote just skin colour, then it must include some of the earliest immigrants to this country—blacks escaping slavery in the United States of America. Giving haven, after all, is one of the grandest of Canadian traditions—one apparently less vital to the Canadian psyche than headgear and a commitment to colour-blindness.

How curious it is, how sad, that at the end of the twentieth century in Canada, elements of the "intelligent right"—as I have heard Mr. Gairdner described—seek a return to the discriminations of the beginning of the century. Urged on by the uncertainties engendered in large measure by multiculturalism policy—expressed implicitly through the use of leavening euphemism—it proposes a racial agenda, a reflection perhaps of the urge to a certain "purity" arising in various parts of the world. This aspect of right-wing thought, then, is different from Yugoslav notions of "ethnic cleansing" only in sophistication and degree. Being Canadian, it is characteristically neither so blatant nor so brutal.

On the subject of multiculturalism itself, Mr. Gairdner poses a number of pertinent questions—how, for example, can cultural diversity be preserved and enhanced when the ultimate goal is, and must be, immigrant integration?—and in so doing, he points up some of the contradictions that make the multicultural policy unworkable.

But his, as I've pointed out, is a vision based on racial homogeneity, and from such a basis flows a series of troubling assumptions and assertions that can be fairly encapsulated in the phrase "Stick with your own kind." He approvingly quotes American journalist James Fallows on the Japanese belief that "a society is strongest when its members all come from the same race or ethnic group."[41] It is a stance that leaves little room for the unity offered by shared experiences, ethics, values.

I would venture that a Canadian of Italian descent and a Canadian of Pakistani descent are likely to have more in common with one another than with Italians or Pakistanis not shaped by the cultural imperatives of this country. Such commonality is not possible, however, if a racial vision leads the way. Mr. Gairdner's approach would suggest that race determines social cohesion. I would suggest, though, that most human beings are not so shallow: that the spirit and the intellect frequently meet in the most unexpected of ways, that brotherhood goes beyond the skin to essential notions of humanity. Simply put: Who makes a better neighbour—a man of any colour who shares your basic values or a man of any colour who does not? Culture, in its essentials, is about human values, and human values are exclusive to no race.

And it is here that multiculturalism has failed us. In eradicating the centre, in evoking uncertainty as to what and who is a Canadian, it has diminished all sense of Canadian values, of what is a Canadian.

In response to the Ekos poll mentioned in Chapter

One, Michael Valpy wrote a *Globe and Mail* column exploring the cultural uncertainty expressed by respondents. He spoke of the fear of losing the old Canada, "a fear on the part of aging Canadians...that the old Canada and its mythologies are slipping away. It is a fear to be found in what [Ekos president Frank] Graves calls a key social indicator: the belief by 60 percent of Canadians that 'too many immigrants feel no obligation to adapt to Canadian values and way of life.' A belief to which all levels of government in Canada contribute by demolishing historic Canadian—to be sure, primarily Euro-Canadian—symbols."[42] He ended the column with the following observation: "Societies are governable either because their members hold important values in common or because their governments have a lot of guns and jails. What efforts do our governments make to promote national values, national symbols, that would allow the country to more comfortably absorb immigrants with different values?"[43]

A reader's response, published on the letters page some time later, revealed the effect of that lack of common values. "I expected Canadians," he wrote, "to regard freedom, honesty, hard work, personal accountability and tolerance as their most cherished values. I am not aware of any immigrant group not subscribing to these ideals. However, I am definitely aware of the millions who cheat on taxes, engage in UI and welfare fraud, expect 42 weeks government handout after 10 weeks employment, indulge in cross-border shopping with false customs declarations, buy smuggled goods, do not feel accountable for their children's poor academic performance or anti-social behaviour, are intolerant to and unwilling to respect the culture of the aboriginals (the 'true' Canadians), and these millions are mostly members of Mr. Valpy's 'old Canada.'"[44]

It is precisely this kind of attitude that engenders resentment—the resentment that causes some to fantasize about "the good old days" and the apparent certainties of homogeneity. The letter-writer is not alone in these sentiments; countless times similar views have been expressed to me by newcomers to the country: the values they seem to encounter here are negative ones. Nor is the writer to be blamed for so ungenerous a view: if those born here have lost their notion of binding values, how can someone, coming from elsewhere, be expected to find them? The letter is informed by a cynicism born of disappointment; it reflects, like all cynicism, a certain pain—a pain that is a mirror image of that felt by members of Mr. Valpy's old Canada: the pain of loss, hurtling into the pain of the never-found, and each resembling a kind of anger.

Both the old Canada and the new, then, pose the same question: What is a Canadian? The answer, elusive for so long, lies in the answer to another, perhaps more pointed, question: What values do Canadians hold dear? In the amorphous present, possibilities compete: the social safety net versus the deficit; bilingualism versus unilingualism; the environment versus the economy; diversity versus homogeneity; nationalist defiance of American values versus former prime minister Brian Mulroney's submission to them. The soul of the country seems to be up for grabs. Ethical decisions must be made.

A place to start would be in accepting that Canadians, because they are of so many colours, are essentially colourless, in the best sense of the word. We can learn from the past—the good old days weren't that good, and they were pretty awful for some—and can begin to construct a new sense of ourselves and our country. To attempt to return wholesale to the past, to seek to shore up superficial traditions, would be pointless, even self-destructive. Canada, I would suggest, has seen enough of that.

Not long ago, I was refused service in the lounge of the Ritz-Carlton Hotel in Montreal. I was unaware that, to sip a gin and tonic in this hotel of esteem and tradition, I had to be appropriately attired. My clothes were most inappropriate. Not only was I wearing jeans but, heaven forbid, I was not wearing a tie either. It was irritating, but funny too, and I took comfort from the recollection that, sometime back in the sixties, a Toronto restaurant of a certain repute had refused admission to Robert Kennedy because of his turtleneck sweater. I hoped that Bobby Kennedy had seen his reception there as I saw mine at the Ritz: as a provincial insecurity camouflaged behind trumped-up notions of a grand tradition.

Jeans and ties are not headgear, but as symbols they strike me as not terribly different, either. They become issues only because the insecurity from which they spring prompts such passion—a passion that itself springs from a desire to maintain control over a little bit of a changing world. In dissecting the results of his company's poll, Ekos president Frank Graves "cautioned against interpreting the trend toward intolerance solely as a function of the economic recession. He said cultural insecurity—the fear that an ill-defined Canadian way of life is disappearing—ranked ahead of economic stress as a key factor in shaping attitudes."[45]

Canada has been for decades a country in transition, and transition entails both gain and loss. The most profound, yet least acknowledged, loss has been that of the old Canada—not just the Canada shaped by racial vision but the country that felt no need to define itself, no need to ask the question "What is a Canadian?" The Canada, in short, that was secure in its sense of its place and role in the world: the Canada that knew itself as firmly part of the British sphere of influence, the Canada devoted to King or Queen, country and, yes, Empire. Ridding ourselves of the British centre may have been necessary, even inevitable. It is part of the mental decolonization of Canada, a country that lags behind even little Bahamas in this respect. While Canadians will still flock to see any member of the royal family, Queen Elizabeth's latest visit to the islands "generated so little enthusiasm that protocol officers rushed to remove several rows of seats before she presided over a ceremony."[46] Even "Third World" countries like India and Trinidad have broken these colonial links, and Australia may do so before too long.

In Canada, the links have not been broken, just severely weakened. It is not a distancing lamented by many: to move away from dependence on a colonial paternalism, to claim the right to make one's own decisions and one's own mistakes, is to be part of the history of the twentieth century. It is part of growing up.

Symbols are an important aspect of growing up—the keys to the car, a room of one's own—and they are an important aspect of transition to full nationhood. Trinidad gained its own flag and anthem in 1962. Canada gained its own flag, after lengthy and bitter debate, only in 1965; and it was another fifteen years, not until 1980, before "O Canada" became the official anthem. Old symbols, the repositories of so much emotion and history, are not easily surrendered. This may be in part because ridding oneself of a colonial *mentality* is so easily confounded with ridding oneself of a colonial *heritage*. Heritage is history: it is there and always will be. The danger comes when heritage paralyzes mentality.

In a country weak in symbols and home-grown traditions, people grow jealous of what they have: simple things become precious. Sometimes the fear of loss can prove paralyzing; it can lead to perception of threat and a rigidity of mind, to the appearance, at least, of intolerance. It is the reason an event such as Pierre Trudeau's patriation of the Constitution in 1982 can be important not only in political terms but also in psychological ones: even with all its flaws, the social contract to which we adhere is one designed by us, for us; it is a declaration of faith in ourselves, a vital political step—however contentious—towards full nationhood, a symbol of ourselves and the vision that shapes us.

But the problem is that the Constitution is a big thing, beyond the grasp of most people. It is unlikely to attain, for individual Canadians, the mythic qualities of the U.S. Constitution for the simple reason that provincial political greed will constantly seek to narrow the vision that informs it. Our Constitution is therefore almost esoteric, with little apparent effect on daily life. Although the *Globe and Mail* received more mail about the Constitution than any other topic, it is still not often *there*, squarely in front of us, an unsettling reminder of change; it is not a visible reminder, in the way that, say, a turban might be, that the centre has disappeared and has left in its ripples a country in flux, a country anxiously asking itself what it is. We experience, therefore, not pride in political and human rights achievement but a cramped resentment of turbans.

It is a basic flaw in the Canadian character, our traditional modesty as a country metastasizing into an inability to see the positive. And so the turban—a length of cloth wound into an object of elegance—becomes a symbol not of what we have gained but of what we have lost.

It is tempting, as many have done, to use adjectives such as "racist" and "bigoted" to describe the self-defence of the old Canada, but it is a temptation best resisted. Name-calling, the application of stereotypical labels, does nothing to advance discussion, and it obscures in vituperative simplicity the true complexity of the question, the larger context of the disappearing cultural centre. In the words of Michael Valpy, "Rightly or wrongly, many Canadians perceive multiculturalism to mean that there is no recognized or protected Canadian culture, a concern to which governments have not responded. If anything, they have turned multiculturalism into a creed of state political correctness."[47] Furthermore, "if we are determined to have multiculturalism, let's make clear that it does not mean neutron-bombing into meaninglessness cultures that have fallen out of political favour. It means sharing everyone's cultures."[48]

The old centre—the centre to which the Ignatieffs came and which has, in Valpy's phrase, fallen out of political favour—is fading fast but not quietly. More than anything else, the cries of "Tradition" that arise from various quarters strike me as the plaintive and somewhat belated battle-cries of the old Canada, a culture once dominant and now battered. It is no longer the centre and, barring mass deportations, this must be accepted as fact, as history: there is no going back.

So—to return to Michael Ignatieff's question—what has changed? The answer, in short, is that the historical centre and the sense of national self it offered are, for all intents and purposes, no more. A void remains, a lack of a new and definable centre. Multiculturalism, the agent of that change and the policy designed to be the face of the new Canada, has failed to acquire shape and shows no sign of doing so. Without a change in focus and practice, it is unlikely ever to coalesce into the centre—distinct and firm and recognizably Canadian—we so desperately need.

Five

The Simplification of Culture

In Canada, I don't think we've really explored how the immigration experience changes people, when they move from one country to another. It's easier just to comment on different foods and folkloric dances than to really understand what people go through when they emigrate.... In Canada, there has been a tendency to trivialize.

Nino Ricci
quoted in *Profiles*
February 1994

It is at times strange to me that for my great-grandparents English was a second language. They were Brahmins, members of the learned cast, but poor. In Trinidad they led tenuous lives working the land, going about their daily tasks—cutting sugarcane stalks, tending rice paddies—mostly in Hindi. That I find this strange says much about the change that the years have brought. Both the lives they led and the language they spoke have now grown impossibly remote, their faces, even their names, long drifted, for my generation at least, into an irretrievable anonymity.

Change, made inevitable by time and space and Bible-toting missionaries from another British colony called

Canada, marked itself on their children. In the schools that bartered education for religious conversion (the bargain not always kept, my paternal grandfather and one of his brothers remaining loyal to the old faith while two other brothers embraced the new), a greater facility in English was acquired. In an agrarian society, this could not have been easy—but forever after, my grandfather ritually read his daily English-language newspaper, lips soundlessly forming the words.

For both my grandfathers, the new language offered escape from the eviscerating labours of the field. My paternal grandfather found success in commerce, while my mother's father, less practical, more of a dreamer, engaged what little literary life the island had to offer by becoming a newspaper reporter who wrote short stories in his spare time.

Success, though, exacted a price. For my father's parents (my mother's father died before I was born), Hindi eventually became little more than a language of religion and secrets, spoken only in prayer and for privacy between themselves. In both families, English, the language of success, was the language of communication with the children, the result being that my parents spoke no Hindi save a word here and there, mostly terms of endearment or disparagement infrequently uttered.

Within three generations, then, the language of my great-grandparents had all but disappeared, and along with it had gone a way of life: dependence on the land, religious belief. We felt no sense of loss, no tincture of regret, no romantic attachment to a language that no longer served the purposes of our circumstance. And those of my parents' generation who still clung to the distant past—the few women who wore only saris, the few men who went to India in search of wives—came to be viewed as eccentric and foolish.

My own world was very different from the one in which my parents had grown up. While, for them, going abroad to study represented a grand and lengthy journey—farewells at the docks, the slow progression of the ship towards the horizon—for my generation it was one more step in a normal progression. Like my contemporaries, my mode of travel was jet-powered, the trip a few short hours. My only language was English, my popular cultural influences, in an island independent only ten years, less British or Indian than American: not Ravi Shankar or Laurence Olivier but the Temptations and Clint Eastwood. Through schooling, I acquired French, Spanish and the cultural influences they entailed, including an enduring love of the poetry of the Spanish poet Federico Garcia Lorca.

When, at the age of eighteen, I left Trinidad for Canada, the journey that had begun in India a century before—and here I mean not just the physical journey—was simply proceeding to its next logical step. (Members of my family now live not only here but in England and the United States as well.) After twenty years, this country now claims all of my loyalty, intellectual and emotional.

India and many things Indian have been left behind. Trinidad and many things Trinidadian have been left behind. Much else, though, has been assumed along the way.

In a way, then, time and circumstance have succeeded where the Canadian missionaries failed—not in terms of religion but in terms of culture. It is a change that can be viewed as a loss to be mourned, but there is, too, a less nostalgic way of looking at it.

In his novel *A Bend in the River*, V. S. Naipaul, my uncle, writes: "The world is what it is; men who are nothing, who allow themselves to become nothing, have no place in it."[1] Making a place for ourselves is what my families have long been good at: it is one of the effects of the fear of becoming nothing. Both families are now replete with doctors and lawyers, teachers and writers. All this has come, in great part, through a refusal to brood over the loss of one language and its cultural baggage and a willingness to fully embrace another. English, then, is not for us a borrowed language but an acquired one, as fully part of my families today as Hindi was a hundred years ago: the distinction is vital.

The languages I speak are central to me. My attachment to them is strong and passionate. They have made me what I am, have provided me with a way of looking at the world, of exploring and understanding it. Perhaps most important of all, they have given me the means of expressing what I see. For in being a writer, in engaging through my imagination the varied elements of familial experience, I am linked to my maternal grandfather and to all of those faceless, nameless people who came before.

Culture is life. It is a living, breathing, multi-faceted entity in constant evolution. It alters every day, is never the same thing from one day to the next. Stasis is not possible. A culture that fails to grow from within inevitably becomes untrue to itself, inevitably descends into folklore.

Culture is a complex entity shaped in ways small and large. A preference for coffee over tea or beer over wine. Movies over books or sitcoms over documentaries. Free-trade over managed trade or insularity over adventurism. Change through negotiation or change through arms. Nothing is inconsequential. Culture must be measured in its minutiae. The very breath of a people must be appreciated, or else that people and their history are trivialized, reduced to the most common of denominators: stereotype.

No consequence of multiculturalism policy is as ironic—or as unintended—as what I would call the simplification of culture.

The public face of Canadian multiculturalism is flashy and attractive; it emerges with verve and gaiety from the bland stereotype of traditional Canada at "ethnic" festivals around the country. At Toronto's "Caravan," for instance, various ethnic groups rent halls in churches or community centres to create "pavilions" to which access is gained through a purchased "passport." Once admitted—passport duly stamped at the door with a "visa"—you consume a plate of Old World food at distinctly New World prices, take a quick tour of the "craft" and "historical" displays and then find a seat for the "cultural" show, traditional songs (often about love in the wheat fields) and traditional dances (often about harvesting wheat) performed by youths resplendent in their traditional costumes. There is tradition in sufficient quantities in these pavilions to satisfy even Tevye, that glutton of tradition from *Fiddler on the Roof* (except that some national traditions never mentioned would see Tevye reduced to a traditional pulp at the hands of mobs driven mad by traditional anti-Semitism).

After the show, positively glowing with your exposure to yet another tile of our multicultural mosaic, you make your way to the next pavilion, to the next line-up for food, the next display, the next bout of cultural edification. It is a kind of journey, not of the "If it's Tuesday this must be Belgium" kind but of the "If it's two o'clock it must be Kiev" kind: a world tour in an afternoon.

And at the end of the day, you may be forgiven if you feel, guiltily to be sure, that you have just sat through a folksy, Canadian-mosaic version of the Jungle Cruise at Walt Disney World in Florida.

It is a sad spectacle, the Jungle Cruise. The guide, in his big-white-hunter outfit, stands at the head of the boat spouting rehearsed wisecracks into a microphone. On shore and in the water—the Amazon, the Nile—mechanical creatures (hippos, pythons, a pride of lions, Indian and African elephants) nod and huff in sightless animation. The guide, cool as a cucumber, fires a cap pistol to "scare off" the threat of a curious hippo.

To accept the reality of these creatures, to be sufficiently taken with them not to feel cheated, requires not imagination but the failure of it. This is nature remade and sanitized, Jungle the Good. It is illusion—and, being from Disney, is not meant to be more. Anyone disembarking from the boat convinced that he has truly experienced the jungles of South America and Africa would be taken for a simpleton.

And so it is with the ethnic cultures offered at the pavilions of Caravan and other such festivals: all the colourful ethnics bowing and smiling in mechanical greeting at the tourists, themselves mostly other ethnics, passing by. They look like the real thing, but their smell is synthetic. They have no bite. They are safe. Culture Disneyfied.

Implicit in this approach is the peculiar notion of culture as commodity: a thing that can be displayed, performed, admired, bought, sold or forgotten. It represents a devaluation of culture, its reduction to bauble and kitsch. A traditional dance performed on a stage is not a people's cultural life but an aspect of it removed from context, shaped and packaged to give a voyeuristic pleasure. It is not without value, but value on par with the reproduced treasures of Tutankhamun sold in every sad store on the continent.

To attend an ethnic cultural festival, then, is to expose yourself not to culture but to theatre, not to history but to fantasy: enjoyable, no doubt, but of questionable significance. You come away having learnt nothing of the language and literature of these places, little of their past and their present—and what you have seen is usually shaped with blatant political ends in mind. You have acquired no sense of the everyday lives—the culture—of the people in these places, but there is no doubt that they are, each and every one, open, sincere and fun-loving.

Such displays, dependent as they are on superficialities, reduce cultures hundreds, sometimes thousands of years old to easily digested stereotypes. One's sense of Ukrainian culture is restricted to perogies and Cossack dancing; Greeks, we learn, are all jolly Zorbas, and Spaniards dance flamenco between shouts of "Viva España!" Germans gulp beer, sauerkraut and sausages while belting out Bavarian drinking songs; Italians make good ice cream, great coffee, and all have connections to shady godfathers. And the Chinese continue to be a people who form conga lines under dragon costumes and serve good, cheap food in slightly dingy restaurants.

There are Chinatowns, it seems, in just about every major city on this continent, benign ghettos (at least to the outsider not prey to gangland extortion) crowded with designer-clad youths and shrunken, combative grandparents. Restaurants, few of which are models of interior decoration or sanitation, jostle stores dense with wicker and plastic; evil-smelling supermarkets offer exotic foods and suspicious-looking herbs. Business establishments are often exquisitely named. I was always particularly fond of the "Happy Meat Market" and the "Wing On Funeral Home," both once on Spadina Avenue in Toronto, and recall with delight the young Taiwanese man who, having decided that he must have an English name, chose Shark, because he admired the animal's tenacity, and when told this would not do chose Ladder, because it symbolized his ambition. He finally settled on Jay, for its beauty and simplicity.

We are proud of our Chinatowns. We show them off to visitors. It is a sign of how far we have come. Once victims of xenophobia, prey to the discriminatory head-tax, the Chinese, whether of Hong Kong, Taiwan or the People's Republic of China, now find Canada, officially at least, a welcoming place. We even have a special immigration program to lure them (or at least their money) here.

But there are problems still, resentments that arise towards any burgeoning group of immigrants, visible or invisible. Some blame the Chinese for the cost of housing in Vancouver; some resent their successes in school, the fashionable clothes, the costly cars.

It was all so controllable before. The Chinese were seen as a silent, hard-working, dispassionate people. They kept mostly to themselves, procreating rather spectacularly, living in tiny, dark rooms, playing mah-jong, gambling in "dens." Now, though, they are going beyond their traditional enclaves, are even unblanding the Toronto suburb of Scarborough with a new Chinatown. And this is profoundly unsettling to those who would rather have their multicultural exoticism safely caged, costumed and staged. We are being forced by events, both here and abroad, to admit that these are people pushing the boundaries of their stereotype. We are being forced to confront their wholeness.

In the early eighties, I earned my living teaching English as a Second Language. At one point, the school welcomed what were still at the time rather exotic creatures: three students, two young women and a man, from the People's Republic of China. They were good students of differing abilities, ready with smiles, as friendly as their command of the language would allow.

One day, as we all sat around having lunch, one of the women began talking about life in China. The words did not come easily to her. She wrestled with the language, passion in her voice, while her compatriots listened blank-faced, adding nothing. But when the words "cultural revolution" spilled with a striking bitterness from her tongue, the man's gaze suddenly bore down on her. In rapid Mandarin, he snapped her harshly into an instant silence—a silence that blanketed the room. Conversation was slow to return in the charged atmosphere.

Back in the classroom that afternoon, the young woman, to my surprise, again took up the theme. This time there was no one to stop her. Within minutes, she was raging about the Red Guard brutality visited upon her father, a doctor; about the destruction of her family; about the poverty in China that allowed children to run around ragged and barefoot, with little education and little food. Her eyes reddened, big tears slicked her cheeks. Her declaration of her intention never to return to China was choked off by sobs catching in her throat. I declared a break while a Venezuelan student offered comfort. When the class resumed a few mintues later, the talk was all of nouns, verbs and adjectives. The subject of life in China was never raised again, but in the quiet classroom in the heart of Toronto her display of rage was rare and, so, unforgettable.

When, some years later, in the spring of 1989, a million demonstrators defied the government in Tienanmen Square; when the brutality of the army was met by the brutality of the protesters; when a man, alone and unarmed, confronted tanks sent to crush his ideals, I heard the rage again, and I witnessed, as did millions of others around the world, the courage of that rage. I saw rage transform forever all notions of the silent and dispassionate Chinese: people seen with greater clarity, people seen in their wholeness. Suddenly, in their hunger for the freedoms we profess to cherish, they were more like us.

So who are they, then, these Chinese people? Their multicultural niche gives us no hint of their passions. If, before, the Dragon Dance evoked hazy background images of restaurants and laundries, it might now offer images of waving banners, excited faces, tanks, gunfire and pools of blood. It might help us to understand that there is more to these people than our exhibitionistic multiculturalism has ever allowed us to appreciate. An honest Chinese pavilion at future ethnic festivals should offer, along with the costumes and the dances and the food, photos and videos of the turmoil in Tienanmen Square—along with honest exposition of the startling economic reforms, instituted by the geriatric government, that are quickly transforming Communist China into Capitalist China. But would this ever happen? Or would such frankness prove too unsettling for Canadian appetites? Maybe the reality is too much. Illusion, after all, is much easier to bear. In the Canadian multicultural context, my former student would, I suspect, find another kind of betrayal, another kind of rage. It is, in the end, a question of respect.

Cultural heritage is not always a pretty thing. It involves the good and the bad, the attractive and the unattractive, reasons for pride and reasons for shame. The brutality of the Red Guards is a vital part of my former student's heritage. It informed, and deformed, her life. It is part of the baggage she brought to this country, an inherent part of herself. She will never forget, she will never forgive. But where do her passions fit in our political concept of multiculturalism? Ours is not a policy that accommodates blood and brutality. We seek only the light and choose to ignore the shadows.

Furthermore, how misleading it is to speak of "the Chinese," as if no radical differences of experience, of outlook, exist between the people of Hong Kong, so long a British protectorate, the people of authoritarian Taiwan and the people of the brutalized mainland. Only through misrepresentation can a place be made in the mosaic for "the Chinese community." Can multiculturalism accommodate the complex reality of these lives? Can it be an unflinching multiculturalism? Or must it inevitably trivialize?

Our approach to multiculturalism encourages the devaluation of that which it claims to wish to protect and promote. Culture becomes an object for display rather than the heart and soul of the individuals formed by it. Culture, manipulated into social and political usefulness, becomes folklore—as René Lévesque said—lightened and simplified, stripped of the weight of the past. None of the cultures that make up our "mosaic" seems to have produced history worthy of exploration or philosophy worthy of consideration.

I am reminded of the man who once said to me that he would never move into an apartment building that housed any East Indian families because the building was sure to be infested with roaches: East Indians, he explained, view cockroaches as creatures of good luck, and they give live ones as gifts to each other. I had known the man for some time, was certain that he was in no way racist—a perception confirmed by the fact that he was admitting this to me, someone clearly of East Indian descent. His hesitation was not racial but cultural. So searching for an apartment, he perceived potential neighbours not as fellow Canadians, old or new, but as cockroach-lovers, a "cultural truth" that he had accepted without question. I was not of India: he would not hesitate in having me for a neighbour. But what would he have done, I wondered later with some discomfort, had he not known me and seen me emerging from a building he was about to visit?

The vision that many of us have of each other is one of division. It is informed by misunderstanding and misconception: often what we know of each other is at best superficial, at worst malicious.

The "Mongolian blue spot" is a light birthmark common to children of Asian and black descent which often disappears as the child gets older. Three-year-old Joshua Ahn and his one-year-old sister Megan were born with Mongolian blue spots. On their first day in day-care in Surrey, B.C., their mother, Jinny Ahn, was informed that they were being detained by day-care personnel and that, furthermore, the RCMP had been called. The children, she was told, had bruises that appeared to be evidence of child abuse. "They told me they suspected me of beating my children," she said. While police contacted the children's doctor, Mrs. Ahn was not permitted to comfort her distraught toddlers.

This was not the first time that Mongolian blue spots had led to problems: in New Brunswick in 1992, three toddlers were abducted by a day-care worker who mistook their spots for bruises. These were certainly honest mistakes prompted by the urge to do good—but is ignorance ever a defence? Mrs. Ahn said, "I think people involved with child care shouldn't be so ignorant of racial differences." They should not be, but it is hardly surprising that they are: we are cognizant of the differences—the shape of the eyes, the colour of the skin—that do not count, but we remain uninformed concerning the ones that do.

Multiculturalism, with all of its festivals and its celebrations, has done—and can do—nothing to foster a factual and clear-minded vision of our neighbours. Depending on stereotype, ensuring that ethnic groups will preserve their distinctiveness in a gentle and insidious form of cultural apartheid, multiculturalism has done little more than lead an already divided country down the path to further social divisiveness.

The Excesses of Sensitivity

It was a case both banal and horrifying. Banal because one would wish such actions less common in our society, horrifying because of the sheer perversity of the act—and also because of the reaction it drew from the trial judge.

On January 13, 1994, Quebec court Judge Raymonde Verreault sentenced a man, unidentified in order to protect the identity of his victim, to twenty-three months in prison for sexual assault. The crown prosecutor had asked for a term of four years. The victim was the man's eleven-year-old stepdaughter. In justifying her leniency, Judge Verreault explained that she had taken the man's religion—Islam—into consideration. The accused, she told the courtroom, had "in a certain manner" spared the victim. She based this conclusion on "the fact that the accused did not have normal and complete relations with the victim—that is to say, vaginal sexual relations, to be more precise—so that he could preserve her virginity, which seems to be a very important value in their religion."[2] The man had preserved the girl's virginity by repeatedly sodomizing her over a two-and-a-half-year period. In view of the man's continued denial of the abuse and his evident lack of remorse, Judge Verreault added, she saw no point in ordering any rehabilitation treatment for him. The defence attorney, while admitting that he found the comments on the lack of vaginal penetration "unbelieveable," also lauded the judge's "very,

very courageous" decision. "She did recognize that there's a value structure,"[3] he told *The Gazette*.

The defence lawyer was right. The judge did recognize the existence of a value structure—but both the defence lawyer and the judge failed to question not only the terms of that structure but its validity as well. Montreal's Muslim community was not alone in its outrage at the use of Islam to minimize what would be a crime in any society. Judge Verreault was subsequently ordered to appear before a hearing into her actions by the Quebec Judicial Council, and so it should be when a judge's competence comes into question.

What is most interesting, however, is Judge Verreault's instinct in deciding on the sentence. Her appreciation of the situation was faulty, her knowledge of Islam inadequate to the task, but she also clearly believed she was being sensitive to the man, to his victim and to the larger ethnic and cultural context. How easily, though, the instinct of sensitivity leads to a loss of perspective. How easily it betrays the urge to do what's right.

It is a lesson the government of Ontario has had to learn.

In November 1993, the Ontario Public Service employment paper *Job Mart* advertised a senior management position for a director of information technology, a job that offered an annual salary of between $74,000 and $111,000. "The competition," the ad read, "is limited to the following employment equity designated groups: aboriginal peoples, francophones, persons with disabilities, racial minorities and women."[4] The ad's approach is positive; it is superbly worded to offer a vision of inclusion. And yet it might have been franker, more honest, had its true message been explicitly spelled out: "White, English-speaking males need not apply." This, of course, would have been too blatant; it would have recalled similar sentiments once directed against Jews and Blacks and Irishmen. So the writer of the ad chose instead to be verbose and circumlocutory, perhaps in the hope that no one would notice that, under the laudable banner of employment equity, the Ontario goverment was implementing a hiring policy not of non-discrimination but of targeted discrimination—and that only one group in society could now acceptably be targeted.

The government of Ontario describes this approach to hiring as one of "positive measures." It has, according to a Management Board memo obtained by *The Globe and Mail*, instituted a program in its various ministries to modify the hiring and promotion process by "limiting competition to designated groups."[5] The program is not limited to the provincial government, however. The employment-equity legislation, Bill 79, applies similar requirements to private companies in order to ensure that "[e]very employer's workforce, in all occupational categories and at all levels of employment, shall reflect the representation of aboriginal people, people with disabilities, members of racial minorities and women in the community."[6] The program aims to establish "goals" and "timetables," but not "quotas," which has become a loaded word. But how is the desired representation to be achieved—how is it to be measured—without a head-count? Without *quotas*? Like the writer of the *Job Mart* advertisement, the defenders of the legislation play linguistic gymnastics—a sleight of tongue, as it were—but no amount of twirling and tumbling can disguise the underlying artifice.

Discrimination is discrimination is discrimination. There is nothing wrong with the word. Life is at its best when there is choice, and choice implies discrimination. We discriminate every day when we choose this newspaper over that one, one lover over another, give to this beggar rather than the next. Sometimes we can verbalize the reasons for our discrimination; sometimes we just go on instinct. But discrimination is always a moral choice; it must be exercised with subtlety: Do I pull into this gas station because its price is better—or because the attendant at the next is black? Do I give change to this beggar because he is an old man battered by life—or to the next because she is a young woman battered by life? I once met someone who left New York City because this moral choice, confronted daily and endlessly, proved overwhelming. But choice cannot be avoided, and in a multiethnic society such as ours, the issue must be confronted. The Ontario government cannot be blamed for trying, yet its approach appears to be yet another instance of sensitivity derailing perspective. The advertisement, quickly mired in controversy, was withdrawn a few days later.

The problem is simple: Is the aim of a hiring program to construct as efficient a public work force as possible, or is to construct a public service that is statistically reflective of the make-up of society? If almost one out of three inhabitants of Metropolitan Toronto is of a visible minority, must one out of three members of the Ontario civil service in Toronto be "visible"? Such a goal, whatever its merits, is not incompatible with the goal of efficiency. What is important is where the stress is placed—on the performance or the appearance. The wording of the *Job Mart* advertisement would suggest that this program stresses the latter: it clearly calls not for the best person for the job but for the best person from the designated groups. The white, male English-speaker who might stand head and shoulders above everyone else in qualification is automatically excluded—and the efficiency of performance is automatically lowered.

Ontario citizenship minister Diane Ziemba said in reaction to the designated-groups controversy, "You might want to do that after many years of failure at bringing people into a workplace. It is one of those temporary positive measures that you might use in an extreme case if everything else has failed."[7] Impatience is understandable. Progress in integrating traditionally excluded groups into the civil service has been slow. But it is now more than ever that patience is required—patience and a stern refusal to compromise on essentials.

Reaching for short-term results at the expense of long-term process serves the goals of ideology—but it serves no one's purposes, least of all the purposes of the designated groups. If it is hateful to be the victim of discrimination because your skin is brown or you must use a wheelchair, it seems to me equally hateful to profit from it—and the attitude of those who would make it so reminds me of those people who go in search of, say, a black lover "for the experience": it is only the skin that attracts, not the person. What may appear open-minded is in fact just another kind of marginalization. It is the attempt to present a restrictive label in the most attractive and respectable light.

It is not impossible to have employment equity—to actively search out and hire those who have been the historical victims of discrimination—without sacrificing the quality of work. A certain amount of discrimination is inevitable, but everything must be done to keep it to a minimum: to force all white, English-speaking males to pay for the wrongs committed by others of their colour, language and gender is like giving an entire class detention because one of its number scribbled a dirty word on the blackboard. It is juvenile and discriminatory.

The ideal in hiring policy, then, would be an initially blind approach, looking only at education, experience and ability: the best person gets the job. But, in the event of parity in those areas, other elements—colour, gender, ethnicity, disability—might justly be engaged in the name of social justice. It is likely that, initially at least, most of those hired will be white anglophone males, but in the long term, as the "designated groups" acquire the necessary tools and qualifications, this too will change. It is not dramatic; it will not purchase votes; but it will in the end serve the goals of ideological belief as well as the needs of the public service and the designated groups.

To adopt the approach of the Ontario government is to breed resentment and to run the risk of rewarding incompetence. It is to create the perception of preferential treatment in the public mind.

On a personal level, as a member of one of those targeted racial minorities, I can think of few things more demeaning to me than to be offered an advantage because of my skin colour. It is demeaning because, no matter what I have struggled to achieve, I am still being judged on the colour of my skin and not simply as a human being with strengths and weaknesses. I am still, even with the best of intentions, being viewed racially—and that is offensive to me.

The same vision seems to have taken hold in education. Hard on the heels of the announcement of an Ontario government policy to encourage high school students to "affirm their racial identity," the University of Ottawa Law School designed an "Education Equity Program" to ensure fairness to "any and all students who feel that traditional examination arrangements are prejudicial to their optimum performance."[8] Since "the examination process with its systemic components may disadvantage some persons," such persons would be allowed to apply for "exam accommodation," meaning that they would be given twice the usual time—in one instance, six hours instead of three—to write their examinations.

While certain of the grounds—illness, religious holidays, physical disabilities—were laudable in their sensitivity, others were, to be generous, certainly creative. Single-parenthood was given by the Dean of Common Law as one instance justifying accommodation on the grounds of "family responsibility": single-parenthood is onerous; time, which childless students can put into studying, must be put into child-care. It is a valid argument, but one that can also be applied to the economically disadvantaged (once known as the poor) who must spend time at part-time jobs that the economically advantaged (still known as the rich) can put into studying.

But it is the grounds of "barriers related to race and culture" that I find both intriguing and creative. What in the world could this possibly mean? It may be a failure of imagination that prevents my understanding. I have searched for a scenario that would justify a student's being given twice the time to complete an examination because of the colour of his or her skin. A cultural scenario worthy of such consideration has also eluded me. But I am quite prepared to offer the benefit of the doubt. The university authorities must have sufficient cause for accepting such grounds.

It is also my imagination, though, that gives me reason for pause. I could imagine myself, sometime in the future, charged with some crime—assault of a literary critic, say—and in need of a lawyer. I make an appointment with a lawyer—of colour, naturally, since I am most comfortable with one of my own—and as I am ushered into his or her office my eye falls on the framed diplomas and I read "University of Ottawa." And my first question for my potential lawyer is whether he or she took advantage of the exam accommodation. Should the answer be affirmative, I immediately take my leave. Lawyers charge $250 an hour. I would rather have an attorney who can deal with my case in half the time, unhampered by "barriers related to race and culture."

Such sensitivities and the policies they engender—whether those of the Ontario government or of the University of Ottawa Law School—serve the interests of no one. They are inimical not only to the society at large, by their possible institutionalization of incompetence, but also to the individuals they affect, by providing such ready excuses. Nothing is as seductive as special consideration: why make the intellectual effort when other factors will ensure success?

That there are problems to be addressed there is no doubt. But simply changing the focus of discrimination, treating members of visible minorities as if their skin colour were a handicap, is no answer. As notions of fairness, such policies are simplistic and disarming. They work against the righting of the wrongs they wish to address and, in doing so, clearly reveal the moral muddle in which we have gone about administering our multicultural society.

Six

The Uses of Ethnicity

> *The cult of ethnicity exaggerates differences, intensifies resentments and antagonisms, drives ever deeper the awful wedges between races and nationalities. The endgame is self-pity and self-ghettoization.*
>
> Arthur M. Schlesinger Jr.
> *The Disuniting of America*

Some years ago, a book-promotion tour took me to Washington, D.C., and to a radio studio where I was to be the guest on a phone-in show. The host and I chatted for a few minutes about my background, my novel, *A Casual Brutality*, and its themes of colonialism, immigration and displacement. I fielded a few calls, answered a few questions—and then I heard through the headphones a soft-spoken young woman calling in to set the historical record straight on the origins of people like myself, people historically and ethnically of India. Of herself she said only one thing, that she was black, and she went on to explain that Indians were a fairly recent invention, the result of a British plot to exterminate the black race not through genocide but through a kind of genetic breeding.

The land called India, she said, had not long ago been populated by Africans. Then one day the English arrived. They took a dislike to the Africans they found and instituted a policy of enforced copulation between Englishmen and black women, the goal being the overwhelming of the black genes by the white genes and, so, the eventual extermination of blacks. The black genes had proven resistant, though, and the rapes instead had produced the people we now call Indians. It was, she explained, the reason that Indians had dark skin with straight, black hair and facial features that appeared a blend of European and African.

I was speechless for a moment and then admitted my ignorance of this version of history—at which point the host's hand gestured a question at me and at my own gestured response, pressed a button for the next call.

Ethnicity is the classification of human beings by race, religion, language, cultural traditions and other traits held in common. Notions of ethnicity allow academics and social engineers to order, and so more easily study, the vicissitudes of the human race. They can, to a point, be useful.

Ethnicity, it must be noted, is not restricted to race alone. Just as "whites" are not ethnics (but Danes, all of whom are white, are), so "blacks" are not ethnics (but Jamaicans, most of whom are black, are). Nor can the black communities of Nova Scotia, people who have lived in this country for as long as the oldest white families, justifiably be considered "ethnic" communities in the popular way—or can they? Moreover, "ethnic" as a synonym for "foreign" or "exotic" or "visible"—as in the term "ethnic food"—is essentially meaningless. I think always with delight of a good acquaintance who, with his traditionally "Canadian" demeanour, likes to complain tongue-in-cheek that he too should be considered an ethnic in view of his Danish heritage—but in the Canadian concept of ethnicity no one is willing to recognize him as such; he's too invisible, he fades into the landscape.

Such categorizations are not without their controversies. They allow the less stable among us to order the human race into ethnic hierarchies (with Jews and blacks usually competing for last place in the ranking of some; with whites in the cellar in the ranking of others). They lend a veneer of respectability to studies such as the one conducted by Professor Philippe Rushton some years ago on the supposed link between penis length and intelligence—a study that suggested that more is not necessarily better. (Guess which ethnic group turned out to be the best endowed and, thus, the least intelligent. Hint: the "results" could be used to explain away the woes of much of the African continent.)

Further controversy arises when it comes to the ethnic/racial breakdown of crime statistics. In 1990, Metropolitan Toronto Police Sergeant Ben Eng broke force policy by collating race and crime data to conclude that the vast majority of crime in the Oriental community was being committed by "phoney refugees" from mainland China and Vietnam.[1] Sergeant Eng's approach was less than scientific—he simply drew conclusions from the names entered in arrest forms and daily occurrence sheets—and so his conclusions attracted a fair amount of outrage (although, tellingly, "30 groups in the Chinese community sprang to his defence."[2]).

Two problems in particular are troubling to opponents of this approach to crime statistics. The first is the question of the actual collection of data. As the head of the Metro Police Services Board, Susan Eng (no relation to the sergeant), asked how far such studies should pursue the racial breakdown: "Are you a Jamaican black, an African black? Are you a Danish white? A Scottish white?"[3] The second problem concerns the use that would be made of the statistics: would they simply be made the basis for official discrimination? As Judge David Cole, chair of the Commission on Systemic Racism in the Ontario Criminal Justice System, so succinctly stated it, "People are torn between 'The truth shall make you free' and 'The numbers will be abused.'"[4]

Perhaps most importantly, though, few opponents subscribe to the belief that firm evidence of a racial/ethnic component in crime and similar bias in the justice system would ever lead to the institution of concrete and positive measures, the only goal that could firmly justify the pursuit of such statistics. Antoni Shelton, executive director of the Urban Alliance on Race Relations, made what seems a remarkable statement in this regard: "Statistics have an academic, not real-life, value and they have political impact on people's lives.... Stats won't dispel the myth that blacks are predisposed to crime. And proving in a lab with numbers that injustice exists won't create the will to do anything about it."[5]

The statement is remarkable for this reason: if statistics of race and ethnicity carefully collected and collated can be used to ensure employment equity, why can they not be used to combat crime? Without the full picture, such policies and programs will always be inadequate—and we deny ourselves the full picture, it seems to me, by denying ourselves certain knowledge because of the fear of misuse.

And, even with the most complete data, even with the most careful and considered application of the results, there would undoubtedly be misuse. Statistics, we all know, are a tool of the devil, easily bent to serve any purpose. A finding of a high percentage of, say, Vietnamese or South Asians involved in criminal activity would surely be used by racists to justify calls for an active and official discrimination. Some abuse is inevitable—but while statistics cannot guarantee the political will necessary to bring about change, neither has fear of inevitable abuse ever prevented the statistical study of social problems and the institution of remedial programs as a result of the knowledge gained.

In the end, though, the larger context provides an uncomfortable perspective: refusing to collect such data is to be untrue to the selves that we claim. It is to allow ethnic communities to have it both ways: to exist as officially protected, promoted and enhanced entities and yet to remain in an important way untouchable, and so subject to abuse from both within and without. Could this explain the decision by at least thirty groups in the Chinese community to defend Sergeant Eng?

Ethnicity can be like a futon mattress; it can cushion and comfort, it can provide a safe and warm place—but the stuffing sometimes shifts, becomes lumpy and irksome, and the lumps must either be accepted or pounded out. Accepting the lumps makes for uneasy sleep. Too often, ethnic communities accept the uneasy sleep. Or, as novelist Joy Kogawa more elegantly put it: "In an age when loneliness, malaise and an overwhelming bigness assail us, our ethnic communities are sometimes no more than bits of driftwood to which a few people cling in the midst of a typhoon. What we need are lifeboats. What we need is Noah's ark."[6]

At the heart of multiculturalism bob these "bits of driftwood": communities shaped by notions of ethnicity; more particularly, by a heightened sense of ethnicity; most particularly, by a heightened sense of their own ethnicity. They are, many of them, what the poet and professor Roy Miki, a Canadian of Japanese descent and a man with a powerful sense of historical grievance, has termed "racialized."

To be "racialized" is to have acquired a racial vision of life, to have learnt to see oneself, one's past, present and future, through the colour of one's own skin. It is not new—*Mein Kampf* hinges on a racial vision; apartheid could not have existed without a racial vision—but it is, in certain circles, acquiring a new respectability as old enemies grow to resemble each other. Nor is this as simple or as agreeable a proposition as it may appear. Ethnicity, race and their permutations are peculiarly conducive to the spinning of fantasy, so that Christopher Columbus becomes merely the evil European who enslaves and massacres noble natives by conquering Paradise; so that the Toronto writer and social activist June Callwood is transformed into a racist; and so that the ethnic genesis of Indians is cast as yet one more nefarious colonial machination.

A sense of one's racial and cultural background, like a sense of one's personal likes and dislikes, is essential to an individual sense of self. Confusion over one's ethnicity, the desperate search for a personal centre and a meaning to one's life, leads to the kind of despair evident in the words of that young woman in Washington. It was clear that her view of history, as peculiar and as misinformed as it was, not only placed her in what was to her a satisfactory historical context, but it also offered the calming notion of herself as a victim of that history. It solidified the nebulous; it soothed the pain of drift. To see oneself in history rather than outside it, to see oneself as a victim of history rather than as one of its victimizers, is to confer on oneself a delicious sweet-and-sour confirmation of one's own existence: deliciously sweet because you cannot be denied; deliciously sour because you have been brutalized. This life you lead is not your fault.

But neither history nor race nor culture is destiny: human beings are saved from that by intelligence and the gift of irony. And it is the ironic eye, questioning, judging, that ultimately refuses to simplify.

Nor does ethnicity guarantee anything in a complex world. Samuel Selvon,[7] Bharati Mukherjee,[8] Rohinton Mistry,[9] Hanif Kureishi[10] and I are all writers, all of the same "ethnicity" to a certain extent, all ethnically "South Asians," all "Indians." Yet I suspect that, as a group, we are at least as dissimilar as similar. Selvon and I were both born in Trinidad, but of different generations and with lives that have followed very different paths to different cities in the same country. Mukherjee, born in Calcutta, found Canada an unhappy place and has built a more satisfying life in the United States. Mistry and I both moved to Toronto from elsewhere and share the experience (with many others) of living and writing in that city. Kureishi, born in England of Indian parents, lives in London: we met once, shook hands, found we had little to say to each other.

Each of these people and I can claim a certain similarity, but we must also acknowledge vastly different contexts, contexts that have shaped personalities sufficiently dissimilar to render the ethnic category, beyond certain superficialities, essentially useless. Selvon remained a Trinidadian all his life. A few years ago, when he was in his mid-sixties and had long been considered a cornerstone of West Indian literature, he said to me, "People keep asking me when I'm going to write my Canadian novel. Man, I'm still dealing with things that happened in my childhood." Kureishi, in manner and imagination, is nothing if not British. Mukherjee has embraced the exuberance of America, while I prefer the quieter pleasures of Canada.

When we meet, it is not as fellow ethnics sharing

unspoken similarities. There is no gravitation around an ethnic bonfire. These are writers whose work I cherish—just as I cherish the work of Kazuo Ishiguro or Ian McEwan or John Irving. I feel a greater affinity for the work of Timothy Mo—a British novelist born of an English mother and a Chinese father—than I do for that of Salman Rushdie, with whom I share an ethnicity. Like those of Gabriel Garcia Marquez, Rushdie's fictions are alien to me. Ethnically, Mo and I share nothing, but imaginatively we share much. In Mo's fictional worlds, as in those of the Peruvian novelist Mario Vargas Llosa, I recognize aspects of myself. As Salman Rushdie once wrote of a similar "community" elsewhere: "England's Indian writers are by no means all the same type of animal. Some of us, for instance, are Pakistani. Others Bangladeshi. Others West, or East, or even South African. And V. S. Naipaul, by now, is something else entirely. This word 'Indian' is getting to be a pretty scattered concept."[11] Scattered, I would venture, to the point of near meaninglessness.

This diversity within the same "ethnic group" is a growing reality in Vancouver, where the "Chinese community" numbers 250,000. It can easily appear monolithic, and yet there are tensions brewing both within the community itself and between the community and others. Raymond Chan, an MP from Richmond, B.C., and secretary of state for Asian-Pacific Affairs, has pointed out the diversity within the community. "Don't look at them as a block,"[12] he has cautioned.

And a block they are not. A clear illustration of this is provided by Shue Tuck Wong, a geography professor at Simon Fraser University.[13] One day, his daughter, a grade nine student, called him a "banana." She explained that other Chinese students, recent arrivals from Hong Kong, Taiwan and China, had called her a banana—yellow on the outside, white on the inside—"because I cannot speak or write Chinese."

A banana: not, then, a real Chinese. It is evidence of arrogance, of a vision informed by notions of racial and ethnic purity. And it was within this context that Professor Wong advised his daughter to respond: "Tell them back that you are a Canadian. If there is anyone who calls you a banana, he must be a racist. It's important you should be recognized on the basis of who you are, rather than what language you speak."

Jim Kwong, a police-community liaison officer who moved from Hong Kong in 1991, offers the "general impression...that many Chinese Canadians who were born here and speak only English prefer to mix with the Canadian mainstream rather than the Chinese community."[14] But language choices are not the only source of division. Business competition is stiff and political disagreements profound. Raymond Chan has alienated many in the Chinese community by organizing protests against the human-rights record of the Beijing government.

Professor Wong is a pragmatic man, a man not blinded by sentimentality: "Learning Chinese is very useful if you are going to make your living in an area that speaks Chinese," he said. "But if you are living in a non-Chinese environment, it's more important to have a good command of the language where you live."[15] It is evidence that Professor Wong has a firm grasp not only on who he is but also on where he is. It is evidence of great personal integrity.

Mr. Chan, who was born in Hong Kong and emigrated to Canada at the age of seventeen, claims no ethnic political base for himself, explaining that part of his motivation in running for office was "to show that even without the support of the [Chinese] establishment, I have the support of the people. I am a Canadian."[16] In the world of multiculturalism, it is a courageous admission.

My point is simple, but it is one usually ignored by multiculturalism and its purveyors—for to recognize the complexity of ethnicity, to acknowledge the wild variance within ethnic groups, would be to render multiculturalism and its aims absurd. The individuals who form a group, the "ethnics" who create a community, are frequently people of vastly varying composition. Shared ethnicity does not entail unanimity of vision. If the individual is not to be betrayed, a larger humanity must prevail over the narrowness of ethnicity.

To preserve, enhance and promote the "multicultural heritage" of Canada, multiculturalism must work against forces more insistent than any government policy. If a larger humanity does not at first prevail, time and circumstance will inevitably ensure that it ultimately does.

When I was in my early teens and already interested in a writing career, I ran into a problem not unfamiliar to every would-be writer: What was I to write about? I soon decided that I, a Trinidadian of East Indian descent (or extraction, as we used to say, making it sound appropriately wrenching) was destined, maybe doomed, to write pastoral stories of dhotied, cow-owning, cane-cutting Hindu peasants in dusty central Trinidad villages.

This was a tall order and the cause of some despair, since I neither knew nor had ever seen any Hindu peasants in dusty Trinidad villages. Having grown up in a modern suburb of Port of Spain to the sounds of Motown, I didn't know whether they even existed. And yet, it seemed to me, I had to tell the story—even if it meant creating it from pure imagination—of an entire community, my community, ethnically inherited, of turbans and woodfires and huts of packed mud and thatch.

This belief, limiting and quickly jettisoned, came from the earnestness of ambition swathed in an idea of race and religion, an idea, finally, of belonging.

Community and belonging: they are at the heart of every immigrant dilemma. In the contentious introduction to her 1985 short story collection *Darkness*, Bharati Mukherjee writes: "In my fiction, and in my Canadian experience, 'immigrants' were lost souls, put upon and pathetic. Expatriates, on the other hand, knew all too well who and what they were, and what foul fate had befallen them."[17] Ms. Mukherjee saw herself as an expatriate, and she began to write of characters equally self-aware, engaging an irony she describes, unflinchingly, as "mordant and self-protective": "Irony promised both detachment from and superiority over, those well-bred post-colonials much like myself, adrift in the new world, wondering if they would ever belong."[18] And then she adds a paragraph that neatly delineates one of the great themes of so-called "immigrant" literature: "If you have to wonder [whether you will ever belong], if you keep looking for signs, if you wait—surrendering little bits of a reluctant self every year, clutching the souvenirs of an ever-retreating past—you'll never belong, anywhere."[19]

Mukherjee looked forward (and not backward) to an idea of immigrant perfection, since found in the United States. It is an idea so alien to the Canadian approach that this country, "hostile to its citizens who had been born in hot, moist continents like Asia,"[20] could not help but seem darker than it probably was at the time.

This wondering, this looking for signs, this failure to belong takes many forms. It is sometimes sad and enervating, sometimes exuberant and colourful. It is always unsettling.

In his novel *No New Land*,[21] M. G. Vassanji explores this theme—a particularly tragic aspect of the immigrant experience—through the story of a man named Nurdin Lalani, his friends, family and community of Muslim Indians exiled to Toronto by the racial politics of Africa.

Vassanji offers a remarkable portrait of the teeming and almost self-sufficient community that has established itself in a large apartment building in the Don Mills section of Toronto. He captures its past and its present, its ambitions and its intrigues, the sounds of its conversations and the smells of its foods: a little society hectic with activity behind tightly closed doors.

Its members make perilous sorties out into the wider society only when they must, usually for work. And who can blame them? For it seems that Toronto offers little beyond humiliation and danger, corruptive peep-shows and physical violence lurking around every corner. When the well-meaning but hapless Nurdin tries to lend a helping hand to a woman in distress, he ends up being charged with indecent assault—merely a pretext for blackmail, it turns out, since the complainant is easily bought off. Even the immigrant haven of Kensington Market holds unholy temptations for Nurdin when he comes close to having an affair with a widowed childhood friend he happens to run into. As a character in another novel by another writer—Nazruddin in V. S. Naipaul's *A Bend in the River*—says about ethnic attitudes in Canada: "The thing about some of those ethnic groups over there is that they don't like moving around too much. They just want to go home as fast as they can and stay there."[22]

The Canadians encountered—all whites, in fact, including a German *fräulein* in Tanganyika who slaps Nurdin's father when his admiring glances grow too frank—reveal a distinct lack of goodwill: any warmth they may display is merely camouflage for their attempts to fleece the newcomers. Only a Montreal immigration officer is friendly, but then his genial "Welcome to Canada" costs him nothing.

These people are, it is clear, Mukherjee's immigrants, put-upon and pathetic. Bitter-sweet descriptions of Dar es Salaam offer a nostalgic vision of the past and make the present seem even darker than it really is, emphasizing the central point that there are, as the title states, no new lands, only new circumstances.

No New Land is a novel, and the community it examines is fictional. But it is fiction based on reality. Such buildings and neighbourhoods are to be found in most major cities of Canada, pockets of ethnicity we choose to honour, as Toronto has done, by erecting street signs in the ethnic lanaguage most prevalent. It makes for the appearance of tolerance and, like the park signs asking visitors to PLEASE WALK ON THE GRASS, good tourist photographs. But Vassanji's description of this community of exiles—so tight, so self-contained, so alienated from the mainstream—is that of an almost classic ghetto. It is not an extreme of multiculturalism but its ideal: a way of life transported whole, a little outpost of exoticism preserved and protected.

And yet one can detect vital changes in the younger generation. Nurdin's teenaged children, for instance, speak a language different from that of their parents, their attitudes—when compared to the young Nurdin in Dar es Salaam—are more independent. The inevitable change, both generational and experiential, is a challenge to the parents—Nurdin interprets his daughter's impatience as a growing hatred of her origins—but the children, it is clear, are leaving behind the ghetto of the mind, their horizons different; Canada for them, unlike for their parents, is indeed a new land. Yasmin, a secondary character, has already found this freedom in the United States, displaying what Mukherjee characterizes as "a movement away from the aloofness of expatriation, to the exuberance of immigration."

If the undeniable ghettoization is bad news for the purveyors of multiculturalism, so too is this uneasy but equally undeniable distancing of the next generation. These children, and their children after them, will in all likelihood shrug off the restraints of ethnicity. They will acquire friends of various backgrounds who share their experience, some of them will intermarry, and most if not all will blend into the mainstream of the society around them, itself already irrevocably changed. They will, in a word, integrate.

Despite the attraction of the past, the changes wrought by immigration and radically different circumstances must be recognized, assimilated and accepted. It is the only way to get on with one's life, the only way to take full advantage of the new possibilities. It is a reality multiculturalism, with its obsessively backward gaze, fails to recognize. Immigration is essentially about renewal. It is unjust, to individuals and to the communities from which they emerge, to require it to be about stasis. To do so is to legitimize marginalization; it is to turn ethnic communities into museums of exoticism.

Marginalization

One never really gets used to the conversation. It will typically go something like this:

> "What nationality are you?"
> "Canadian."
> "No, I mean, what nationality are you *really*?"

There is probably not a person who has emigrated to Canada from a hot, moist country who has not been asked: "Why in the world did you come here, to this cold and beachless land, from *such a beautiful place*"? It is a question simplistic in the asking; it assumes so much. But it is also a question breath-taking in the response; it ignores so much.

Your first thought, as you take a deep breath, is: What does this person, fantasizing about perpetual sunstroke, want to hear? A cry of desperation? *Yes! Yes! God, why have I done this to myself?*

Your second thought is: Don't you read the newpapers? Don't you know what's happening in the world?

And your third thought, in growing desperation, is: Where do I begin?

No obvious point of departure offers itself because you know that your reasons for leaving "such a beautiful place" are so complex that your questioner would require a whirlwind tour of history, politics and economics all mixed together with a healthy dose of reality. So you simply plunge ahead, hastily tossing out words—depending on where you come from—like "political corruption," "torture," "violence," "murder," "oppression," and you watch your questioner's eyes glaze over, his gaze grow distant, his face tighten into a barely restrained scepticism. He has seen tourist posters, he has watched "Travel, Travel" on television, he subscribes to *National Geographic*. And you know that your words are competing hopelessly in his head with stylized visions of sun, sea and sand, that your version of reality cannot hope to vanquish the Tropics à la Club Med.

Should you manage to complete your answer—and more often than not the reception proves too disheartening halfway through—you frequently run into the stunningly unanswerable: "Yes, but we have all that in Canada, too...."

You nod, despite the obscenity of the remark which, in its ignorance, in its heartlessness, devalues so much

Third World pain, so much Third World struggle; for to reject this assertion is to lose all hope of convincing your questioner that, in coming here, you have immeasurably improved your lot—and it is suddenly vital that you do so. You need to narrow that gap; you need to prove that your decision to move here was neither whimsical nor erroneous. Yes, you agree, there is political corruption in Canada, and violence and murder—isn't there everywhere?—and the native peoples may have something to say about oppression and torture of a kind, but.... You offer the merest of acknowledgements, for, in the end, the conversation is really about the weather.

So you talk about growing up in the hot, moist country. You talk about the heat and the humidity and the sensation of physical oppression. You tell of sitting and reading and, with no greater physical exertion, of sweating like a pig. You tell of laboured breathing, of your energy drained and the soporific effect of the air itself. You dramatize: A hurricane hit the island once ...

But winter! comes the response. All that snow, all that slush, the bite of the wind on your nose, ears, teeth: the endless inhumanity of it all!

You reveal your perversity: You enjoy winter. No, you don't ski, you haven't quite managed to get the hang of skating, you don't even enjoy watching hockey. But you need less sleep during the winter months, your concentration improves, your productivity goes up, your sense of well-being is sweetened.

But you can't go outside in shorts and a T-shirt the way you can in "your" country ...

There's no point in explaining that Canada is now your country—you have been distanced from the beginning, seen merely as some exoticism on two legs—so you remark that to go outside in "my" country is often to enter a sunlight strong enough to crisp your skin, a heat so powerful it causes you to shiver even as it sucks your strength out through your pores. So, if you can afford it, you prefer to stay indoors, shut off from the sweltering world in a room defined by shadows and the hum of an air-conditioner.

But isn't winter equally imprisoning? Who wants to go out into a world that resembles a freezer gone wild?

The point, though, is that with the proper clothing you can, whereas the portable air-conditioner has not yet been invented.

But for your questioner, caressing images of coconut trees swaying in the breeze, all of this is beside the point. He has been to the Bahamas or Jamaica or Cuba; he has experienced life in the islands, life lived on the sand.

And this is the crux of the problem. Experiencing the tropics only as a two-week visitor, passport and return air-ticket safely tucked away in a pocket, he can afford to speculate on the leavened delights of life in tropical zones. But you grew up there, you consider the experience from a rather different point of view. So the simplistic question brings two completely opposed visions hurtling towards one another. Yet you pursue the answer because the question itself is mildly insulting; it assumes your philosophy of life and your urge to accomplishment are sufficiently shallow that you would choose your country of residence based on mere meteorology.

So, despite the beauty left behind, you look fondly on the blowing snow, the frigid wind and the treacherous ice of February. You smile to yourself, you smile at your questioner, for you know that all this, even with its challenge, is symbolic of a greater freedom than you have ever known.

Your questioner smiles back and, after a moment of silence, asks what food people eat in "your" country.

Pizza, you say. Big Macs, Kentucky Fried Chicken ...

To be simply Canadian, untinged by the exoticism of elsewhere, seems insufficient, even unacceptable, to many other Canadians. The fact clearly stems, in part, from the simple human attraction to the exotic. But it seems to me that it also has much to do with a wider issue: the uncertainty we feel as a people.

We reveal this uncertainty in a variety of ways, including our newly minted concern for traditions, but particularly through that quintessential (and possibly eternal) Canadian question: Who are we? The usual answer—"Well, we're not like the Americans ..."—is insufficient: a self-perception cast in the negative can never satisfy (although it can obsess: in John Robert Colombo's *The Dictionary of Canadian Quotations*, "Canada" requires fewer than nine columns while "Canada & the United States" fills more than seventeen).

Nor might we be pleased by the impression offered of Canada by Naipaul's Nazruddin: "I felt the place was a hoax. They thought they were part of the West, but really they had become like the rest of us who had run to them for safety. They were like people far away, living on other people's land and off other people's brains, and that was all they thought they should do. That was why they were so bored and dull."[23]

American novelist Alison Lurie's take is more personal: "[H]e wasn't hateful, or cruel, or cold-hearted, or neurotic. But he seemed to be...I don't know...a Canadian."[24]

There are many visions of us, many answers to that question of who we are, some complimentary, some critical. And so, ourselves lacking a full and vigorous response ("A Canadian," the English essayist J. B. Priestley once remarked, "is lost when he asks himself what a Canadian is."[25]) we search for distinctiveness—exoticism—wherever we can find it. And we find it most readily in our compatriots most recently arrived.

For people I think of as "professional ethnics"—they who enjoy the role of the exotic and who depend on their exoticism for a sense of self—this is not an unpleasant state of affairs. But for those who would rather be accepted for their individuality, who resent being distinguished only by their differences, it can prove a matter of some irritation, even discomfort. The game of exoticism can cut two ways: it can prevent an individual from being ordinary, and it can prevent that same individual from being accepted.

Trudi Hanley, a twenty-one-year-old black woman who works in a field—modelling—where exoticism can reasonably be expected to be an advantage, once spoke to a reporter of the excuses used by those reluctant to hire her: "My nose was too big. I was too black. I was too different. We have enough ethnics. I heard them all."[26]

But the finest example of this exclusion remains the sprinter Ben Johnson. Within a shattering twenty-four-hour period in Seoul, Korea, Mr. Johnson was transformed in media reports from being the Canadian who had won Olympic gold through effort to the Jamaican immigrant who had lost it through use of drugs. The only thing swifter than Mr. Johnson's drug-enhanced achievement was his public demotion from "one of us" to "one of them." The exotic multicultural concept of the everlasting immigrant has come to function as an institutional system for the marginalization of the individual: Ben Johnson was, in other words, a Canadian when convenient, an immigrant when not. Had he, success or failure, been accepted as being simply Canadian and not "Jamaican-Canadian," it would have been difficult for anyone to distance him in this way.

Thus the weight of the multicultural hyphen, the pressure of the link to exoticism, can become onerous—and instead of its being an anchoring definition, it can easily become a handy form of estrangement. Dr. John Polanyi, born elsewhere, is the *Canadian* Nobel-prize-winning chemist. Michael Ondaatje, born elsewhere, is the *Canadian* Booker-prize-winning novelist. Valery Fabrikant, born elsewhere, is the *Russian émigré* murderer.

This hyphen, even when it is there in spirit only, is a curious beast. It appears to mean so much and is yet so often indicative of so little.

Ali Sharrif, a Somali immigrant who freelances for *NOW* magazine in Toronto, began wondering why the city's black community had failed to come to the aid of Somalis in conflict with long-time residents of six apartment buildings in Toronto. He telephoned a man identified only as a "well-known Toronto black activist" and was told, "You see, it's hard to place the Somalis. They really are not black in the true sense of the word."[27] He explained that the black community in North America saw Somalis and other people from the Horn of Africa as Muslims and Arabs first, Africans second. Somalis, who to those without the distinguishing eye bear a strong resemblance to Ethiopians, are Muslims but not Arabs, Africans but not black, and in Metro Toronto they find acceptance and support difficult to obtain. Sharrif ends his article on a note that is part plaintive, part angry: "Most of the Somalis I know, casual acquaintances and friends, really want to be part of the black community. But their fate might be that they are considered black, but not black enough to be really black."[28]

Too much of this, not enough of that: it is a problem. There are people of African descent, born in the Caribbean, immigrants to Canada, who describe themselves as African-Canadians, a phrase now deemed more acceptable than "coloured" or even "black." Yet I cannot help wondering how, say, former South African president

F. W. de Klerk would be described should events force him to flee his country for a Canadian haven: would he too be an African-Canadian? And what about, say, Muammar al-Qaddafi? Libya too is in Africa. I am uncertain, then, as to the precise meaning of phrases such as African-Canadian or Italian-Canadian or Greek-Canadian, particularly when applied to people whose experience of these foreign lands is most likely historical, touristic or anecdotal: what conclusions are to be drawn from them? Their principal effect, I would suggest, is not to define the word "Canadian" but to mark a distance from it, the hyphen that links them a sign of an acceptable marginalization.

If the questions of degree of race and ethnicity, and of that troublesome hyphen, unsettle me, it is because they strike close to home—as they strike close to home for the growing number of Canadians whose personal relationships entail a commingling of ethnicities. It is a realm that must be entered with care, for the very language we use is a minefield of offence.

One of my favourite *New Yorker* fillers—those little nuggets of linguistic curios with which the magazine rounds out its articles—concerned a U.S. newspaper that reported on the restructuring program instituted by a faltering company. Not only would the plan save jobs in the long run, the newspaper reported, but it was expected eventually to put the company's books back in the African-American.

Back in the *what*?

The newspaper subsequently ran a correction explaining that it had meant to say that the company's finances would be back in the—uhh—black. It blamed overzealousness on the part of a copy-editor.

The trend to more specific ethnic self-identification is a complex one. What is one to make, for instance, of Sir

Peter Ustinov, he of the Russian surname, the British manner (Jacques Parizeau with a sense of humour and no chip on the shoulder) and a family history that ties together influences from Russia, Italy, France, Germany, Switzerland and, by virtue of a great-great-grandmother, Ethiopia (which may qualify him as a person of colour)?

A similar deconstruction would make of me an Indian-West-Indian (or, more accurately, an Indian-Trinidadian-West-Indian) by birth and an Indian-Trinidadian-West-Indian-Canadian by choice. My companion's ethnicity is less complex. She would be a Franco-Québécoise-Canadian (barring possible confirmation of a family legend that tells of an infusion of native blood somewhere in the distant past).

But what then of our daughter?

With her mixture of heritages, should she one day be asked to define her ethnicity, she would be obliged to take a deep breath before replying that she is "a Franco-Québécoise-First Nations-Indian-Trinidadian-West-Indian-Canadian." Or something of the sort. (I am assuming here that the actual order of the ethnicities is not subject to political considerations, but I may be wrong.) I do shudder, though, for the children she may one day have should she choose to have a family with someone of different but equally complex composition.

There is an interest here, it seems to me, in a certain simplicity, a simplicity that my daughter might find in moving away from an ethnic concept of self-definition (without abandoning the knowledge of it) towards a self-definition based on her homeland. But, as I found out after the publication of an article I wrote on the subject, even the word "homeland" is problematic.

I had written in the article of the many young men, born and bred in Canada of parents from Croatia, who had returned to that unhappy land to take up arms in its defence. I was puzzled by their actions, concerned about the implications for Canada, saddened by the thought of young men eager to go off to war. The following week, a Montreal writer and editor named François Hébert penned a reply to my piece in which he defended the right of these young men to go to the aid of, as he put it, their homeland. I had not questioned their right, but what struck me in the reply was the defining of Croatia as the "homeland" of these young men.

My understanding of the word would have defined Croatia as the homeland of these young men's parents or grandparents, while their homeland would be Canada, the land of their birth and upbringing. I felt that to view their *ancestral* land as their homeland was to wilfully distance them, to make them marginal to the Canadian context. It was to define the belonging of others through the prism of one's own personal and political needs, in a way not very different from the historical view of that young woman on the phone-in show in Washington.

To consider the ancestral land as the true homeland is to risk engaging a dizzying absurdity, for it would mean that my homeland is India, a place I have never visited and have little wish to. It would mean that Lucien Bouchard's would be neither Quebec nor Canada but France; Brian Mulroney's would be Ireland, David Suzuki's Japan, Nino Ricci's Italy and so on. Only aboriginals, then, could claim Canada as their homeland—unless it is true that they happen to have migrated here thousands of years ago from another continent, in which case they're out of luck. And what is one to make of the homelands of people like Pierre-Marc Johnson, Claude Ryan, Jeanne Blackburn and others complicated by history?

And what of my daughter's homeland? Does she have two, India and France? How much time must go by, then, how many cultural changes are required, before one's homeland is no longer that of one's ancestors? Is there a moment when one stops being, in the eyes of others, an alien, an exile, an immigrant?

It seems to me vital that, as unfashionable or as outdated as it may seem to some in their rush both to claim and to impose narrow ethnicity and tribal exoticism, that my daughter should grow up to think of her homeland as simply Canada and of herself as simply Canadian. In this way, there will be no other "homeland" to which others can wilfully consign—and therefore distance—her, alienating her from the mainstream and thereby withholding her rightful place in the land of her birth.

There is also a strong element of marginalization in the Sikh-turban issue. The controversy of turbans in Legion halls and in the RCMP is in itself an indication of the failure of multiculturalism programs to go beyond superficiality in explaining us to each other. To view the turban as just another kind of hat, with no significance beyond sheltering the head, is to say that a cross worn on a chain is of no significance beyond a decoration for the neck: it is to reveal a deep ignorance of the ways and beliefs of others. To ban either in any context is to revel in that ignorance and to alienate the wearer by rejecting an intimate and fundamental part of his or her self.

The marginalization to which we so easily subject one another comes frequently in times of economic hardship. The stresses of unemployment—the difficulty of the present and the unimaginable idea of a future—create a need for scapegoats: we need something or someone to blame. We can rail against politicians, taxes, corporations—but these are all distant, untouchable.

No one is more easily blamed for the lack of opportunity than the obvious "foreigner" cleaning tables in the local doughnut shop or serving behind the counter at McDonald's. Maybe he has brown skin, maybe he speaks with an accent: clearly he is out of place here, filling a paid position that should by rights have gone to a "real" Canadian. All differences, always so close to the surface, are seized upon, turned into objects of ridicule and resentment, the psychology of exoticism once more cutting both ways.

Encouraging people to view each other as simply Canadian, discouraging the use of the marginalizing hyphen, would not solve such problems—humans, in times of fear and anger, have a unique ability for seeking out bull's-eyes in each other—but it might help deflect some of the resentment, so that in expressing our pain we do not also alienate our fellow citizens. Differences between people are already obvious enough without their being emphasized through multiculturalism policy and its growing cult of racial and ethnic identity.

Divided Loyalties

Not only through marginalization, though, does the game of ethnicity work counter to the best interests of ethnic groups. It inevitably has an effect on their own psychology as well, on the way they see themselves and their place in the world.

> TORONTO—John Sola, a Liberal member of the Ontario legislature who is of Croatian descent, has rejected demands that he apologize for telling a CBC television interviewer: "I don't think I'd be able to live next door to a Serb." Mr. Sola said he made the comment to stress that he cannot accept arguments of Serbian extremists that they will not feel secure until they eliminate all Croations. The Canadian Serbian Council is demanding his resignation.
>
> *The Globe and Mail*, December 7, 1991[29]

When, some time ago, Yugoslavia was beginning its inexorable slide into horror, a CBC news report stated that an estimated 250 sons of Croatian immigrants, young men of able body and sound mind, had left the country to take up arms in defence of Croatia. The report prompted a question: How did these young men define themselves? As Croatians, or Croatian-Canadians? As Canadians of Croatian descent, or Croatians of Canadian birth? And I wondered which country they would choose if one day obliged to: the land of their parents, for which they had chosen to fight, or the land of their birth, from which they had chosen to depart?

It seems an unfair question. Not only does federal law accept the concept of dual citizenship—which implies an acceptance of dual loyalties—but Canadians themselves have a long and honourable history of inserting themselves into foreign wars. Dr. Norman Bethune is just one among hundreds of Canadians, for instance, who enlisted in battle on the republican side of the Spanish civil war.

But Yugoslavia in the 1990s is not Spain in the 1930s: the situations differ in their essentials. While Spain saw foreign youth taking up arms in defence of an idea, in Yugoslavia foreign youth have taken up arms in defence of ethnicity. While Spain's was an ideological conflict—the pull of ideas—Yugoslavia's is tribal—the pull of blood: the distinction is vital.

To forsake one's country, to commit oneself to battle in the land of one's forebears for ideals not intellectual but racial, is at best to reveal loyalties divided between country and ethnicity. The right to decide on the distribution of one's commitments is, of course, fundamental: freedom of belief, freedom of conviction, freedom of choice. It says much about the new country, however, that its command of its citizens' loyalties is so frequently tenuous.

Divided loyalties reveal a divided psyche, and a divided psyche, a divided country. These young Canadians of Croatian descent are not alone in their adulterated loyalty to Canada. Others, too, find it impossible to make a whole-hearted commitment to the new land, the new ideals, the new way of looking at life.

Imported Old World feuds—ethnic, religious and political hatreds that have simmered for centuries in lands both hot and cold—frequently override loyalties to the new country. If the aiming of a gun at one's traditional, Old World enemies breaks the laws of Canada, so be it: the laws of Canada mean little against the older hatreds. And multiculturalism, in encouraging the wholesale retention of the past, has done nothing to address what is a serious—and has at times been a violent—problem. In stressing the differences between groups, in failing to emphasize that this is a country with its own traditions, ideals and attitudes that demand respect and adherence, the policy has instead aided in a hardening of hatreds. Canada, for groups with resentments aroused and scores yet unsettled, is just another battleground. Mr. Sola, the Liberal MPP, does not see other Canadians when he assesses potential neighbours; he sees Serbs. He does not see fellow Canadian citizens; he sees, instead, ancient European enemies.

Writing of the conflict in Northern Ireland—yet another European antagonism that has crossed the Atlantic—*New Yorker* writer David Remnick commented: "To be visionary means to throw off the weight of history and take advantage of what few openings exist."[30] This is never an easy step to take—it requires, above all, a leap of faith and imagination—but it is one that, in a new context far from the blood-soaked soil, is not impossible either. A new country can provide that context; it is up to individuals to provide the faith and the imagination. Romeo and

Juliet had to die because their faith and their imaginations were betrayed by the passions of their parents.

The insistent vision of historical resentment, passed down to the next generation, has already led—and will continue to lead—to suspicion, estrangement, vandalism, physical attack and death threats. It is yet another aspect of the multicultural heritage we seek to preserve, promote and share—but are hesitant to confront.

The Romance of the Past

She was a bright and elegant young woman, a member of a distinguished eastern European family that had been exiled by failed revolution and Soviet tanks. She knew her history—she could point out the names of ancestors in the history books—and she spoke her ancestral language with ease and fluency.

There was a story she liked to tell. It was a tale of upheaval and danger, of her grandmother's desperate preparations for flight, preparations that included the problem of the family jewels: was it better to take them along or hide them somewhere so they could be retrieved in safer times? Her grandmother decided that the journey to safety would be too perilous, the opportunities for loss too great. And so this elegant and sophisticated woman stole out into the garden late at night and, probably for the first time in her life, wielded a shovel. She then fled to a new life in a land much farther away than she had anticipated.

The safer times, which the grandmother expected would come in a matter of weeks or months, took decades. And, in the granddaughter's telling, the jewels were in all likelihood still buried deep in the earth in a corner of the small garden in the ancient city, waiting to be exhumed and returned to their rightful owner. It was the ideal historical romance.

Romance is not in itself a bad thing; it is an edited and prettified version of the past. It makes for a good story. But romance is legend, and legend is not reality. The granddaughter sometimes spoke of the jewels, and of their retrieval, in a manner that suggested the stringency of fact. I hoped that, even given the opportunity, she would not attempt to write a sequel to her grandmother's story, for there could be no sadder chapter to her life, it seemed to me, than a shovel, that garden in the ancient city and the earth upturned in search of the family jewels.

Yet many do go. They go "back," they go "home." They go to a place where the sun shines more brightly, where the grass is greener, the air sweeter. They go to where the family jewels lie buried, to what they feel to be the source of their souls.

Some go to take what a friend once called "the $6,000 cure," the apocryphal cost of the return "home" that, more often than not, buries nostalgia under reality. For many, the journey is inevitable: establishing oneself in a new land is always difficult; the effort can make the land left behind seem idyllic, and often only renewed contact will evoke the reasons for the initial departure and at last cast the new land and the life it offers in a sharper, more compelling light. It is a sentimental journey that many, even most, immigrants must make before they can truly move on with their lives.

Others, though, go back, go home, with more serious purposes in mind. They go, shovel in hand, in search of those metaphoric family jewels. They invest in a sacramental journey towards a fabled treasure which, precious in the telling, turns frequently to paste in the hand.

An article filed from Riga, Latvia, published in *The Wall Street Journal* and reprinted by *The Globe and Mail*,[31] contained the following quote from a Mr. Ilmars

Lejins, a twenty-two-year-old Swede of Latvian descent: "I was raised to be here [Latvia]. I'm not a Swede, I'm a Latvian. Just because you're born in a barn doesn't mean you're a horse." The metaphor is strikingly wounding—Swedes might not take kindly to having their country compared to a barn, and themselves to horses, by a young man born of parents to whom they had given refuge from political chaos—but it leaves no doubt as to the young man's attitudes. Latvians in exile have long been noted for their nationalism and the passion they have brought to the cause of national liberation, but the metaphor of the horse and the barn is one shared by many peoples in many different lands. Many young Canadians of Croatian and Serbian descent, for instance, would nod in understanding and approval.

The article also tells of the travails of several Canadians of Latvian descent who have returned to the newly independent land with "stories about amber shores and large family homes with servants' quarters" and talk of Riga being the "Paris of the North" dancing in their heads, only to find that "the land of their ancestors has streets paved with disappointment." "We're suffering here," said one, who had moved his family from a spacious Ottawa home to four rented rooms in a crumbling house. "We're out of our element." His wife added, "Moving here was such a shock."

Others, though, have found a certain measure of success despite having to deal with everything from protection rackets run by the Russian mafia to street violence to hospitals inhabited by cats and cockroaches and "toilet paper so stiff it can double as stationery." One man, a lawyer from New York, said, "We're making a difference." Another, a bar owner from Toronto, said, "It's the wild, wild East. There's money to be made."

Native Latvians, though, seem to be ambivalent at best

about the newcomers. Obliged, as foreigners, to pay ten times the rental market rate for their four rooms, the Ottawa couple find little sympathy: "That's the way it should be," they're told. And the deputy editor of the country's largest newspaper, *Diena*, said, "Some really want to help us rebuild the state. But at the same time, it seems some have come only because of their big ambitions." The newcomers may see themselves as Latvians, but the Latvians remain suspicious, and making friends is difficult.

Michael Ignatieff ran into a similar situation in the Ukraine, where he encountered numerous Canadians of Ukrainian descent come "home," bright and personable young people, well-meaning, but possessed of an unmistakable arrogance. In *Blood and Belonging*, he tells of meeting a young Canadian journalist of Ukrainian descent who explains that "[i]t is common...for Canadian Ukrainians to think of themselves as the true Ukrainians, the ones who kept the faith while among the actual Ukrainians the compulsion and fatalism of the communist system was working its way into their bones."[32] The newcomers found not "a fervently nationalist and religious people" but "phlegmatic, ironic, sober and fatalistic Soviet souls," and she suggests that independent Ukraine requires "a new human type," a phrase that uncomfortably echoes early Soviet aims of remaking humanity into "Soviet man."

What is striking in all of this is that it seems to have escaped the attention of the Canadians that their conception of Ukrainian culture has been affected, altered, "deformed" by the Canadian, North American context just as much as the native culture was affected, altered, "deformed" by the Russian/Soviet context. These young people, technologically minded and professional, are as distant from nineteenth-century farmers and Cossacks as native-born Ukrainians are distant from the Canadian-Ukrainian concept of "true" Ukrainianism. Both have been remade by the circumstances of history, and what the Canadians encounter is not so much the shock of recognition as the shock of strangeness.

There is, in the novel *Schindler's List*, a short but wonderfully telling scene towards the end when Oskar Schindler and his escort of Jews, having fled from the advancing Russians towards the American lines, encounter a group of Jewish infantrymen accompanied by a field rabbi. There are rounds of applause, handshakes, embraces: "The young GIs seemed so open, so loud, so childlike. Though one or two generations out of Central Europe, they had been so marked by America that the Schindlers and the prisoners looked at them with as much amazement as was returned."[33]

Expecting to recognize themselves, young Canadians in the Ukraine instead encounter themselves as they might have been—and the image is unwelcome. To talk of the need to construct a "new human type," then, is simply to express the desire to remake the native-born in the image of the foreign-born. It is one response to disappointment.

"Many immigrants," Nino Ricci has pointed out, "hold onto romantic visions of their country which has changed dramatically since they left, and this contributes to a distortion of their identity. In their own country, they would have evolved with the customs of that country. And here, they hold strong to this idealized traditional notion of their culture."[34] A notion that cannot help but be, to a great extent, fanciful and so, without caution, misleading.

In the early sixties, V. S. Naipaul undertook a similar, if less ambitious (he did not harbour the illusion of permanent return), journey to his ancestral land, India. He travelled around for a year grappling with the immensities of the land, recording his impressions, admitting finally that India had failed to seduce him, that it had remained for him "an area of darkness."[35] He had learned what he termed his "separateness from India."

At the end of his sojourn, and principally from a sense of duty, he paid a visit to the village from which his father's family had departed more than sixty years before. The visit distorted his sense of time: he heard stories of his grandfather; he was shown sepia photographs bearing the stamp of a Trinidad photographer. The context was strange to him: he was unfamiliar with the etiquette and had to be guided through it; he needed the services of a translator. But it proved an exhilarating experience—until a distant relative he had not seen during the visit turned up at his hotel the following day.

He was an old man, ill and malnourished. He brought offerings—rice, *parsad*—and insisted, endlessly, on having Naipaul in his hut for a meal: "I want to see you there. I want to talk to you. I have important things to say to you."[36] Naipaul returned to the village a few days later. The man was waiting for him. What was so important? The old man had a problem; the problem could be solved through litigation; litigation cost money, and he was short of cash. Naipaul refused. The old man said the litigation concerned him: it concerned the land his grandfather had owned in the village, the land that had produced the rice he had offered at the hotel. Some of that land was in danger of being lost—and if that happened, "Who will look after your grandfather's shrines?"[37] Forget the litigation, forget the shrines, Naipaul replied. Concentrate on the land. But the old man was insistent. Naipaul had to walk away, an abrupt and unpleasant departure.

The episode is a painful one to read, as it must have been a painful one to recount: it is so full of distress and ugliness. It can be read as an account of attempted blackmail, the past—the grandfather's land, the grandfather's shrines—held up as financial and emotional obligations.

There is no doubt that to find yourself for the first time in your ancestral land, surrounded by a people and a landscape that speak wordlessly to your soul, can be for many a powerful emotional experience.

It can be wrenching: "It was a journey," Naipaul writes of his first Indian experience, "that ought not to have been made; it had broken my life in two."[38] It can be fulfilling: "These are all my people," said an Englishwoman of Latvian descent to the *Wall Street Journal* reporter. Michael Ignatieff himself, born in Canada, resident in England, writes feelingly of his visit to the family graves in the Ukraine; and yet, "[y]ou come away from the Ukraine believing that all the rhetoric about nationhood, about the return to Europe, is very distant from the quotidian reality...; it is easy to import videocassettes and blue jeans and condoms and hard currency restaurants, but so much more difficult to import Western habits of mind and reconcile them with a Ukrainian way of life, to fuse them with a vision of belonging to the here-and-now."[39]

The soil and the air that nurtured generations may touch, in ways inexpressible, some deep recesses of the mind: it is a purity of feeling that is distinctly human. But it is, at the same time, illusory to assume that this soil, this air, mark the place where you belong. That they are yours there is no doubt—but they are yours only vicariously. It is like the young woman telling the tale of her grandmother's buried jewels: the legend is hers; the jewels are her grandmother's. The reality is not lost on many of the newcomers in Riga: few have surrendered their other citizenship, and the Ottawa couple have rented out their suburban home for only one year—their airplane tickets are round-trip, with an open return.

Shared ethnicity guarantees neither fellowship of feeling nor congruity of interest.

Shared ethnicity, in fact, guarantees nothing.

The round-trip ticket, the Canadian passport: there is another angle from which this phenomenon may be viewed.

Citizenship, whether through birth or naturalization, implies belonging. It implies a basic commitment of intellectual and emotional loyalty. It is a thing of value. And yet, in recent years, the diminishing value of Canadian citizenship—the creation of the hyphenated Canadian with divided loyalties, the perception that immigration policy now permits the rich to buy their way into the country, the idea that citizenship is a matter of rights and not of obligations—means that the opposite has also come to be true. Canadian citizenship is frequently seen not as a means of committing oneself to the country but simply as a way of abandoning it with an assurance of safety.

Few passports are safer than a Canadian one; it opens borders and doors that an American one will not. It carries no legacy of political or colonial resentment. For many people, as a result, Canadian citizenship merely means access to a passport that allows return to the (dis)comforts of the former or ancestral homeland with the assurance of safe haven should plans go awry, or should political instability necessitate flight.

In the mid-1970s, as a result of policies instituted by the Organization of Petroleum Exporting Countries (of which it was not a member), Trinidad's oil reserves caused the island to rise from a debtor nation to a regional lender, the fantasy of sudden wealth realized through the efforts of others far away. The pressure to return "home"—always with the best of intentions: to do my bit, to help my people, to contribute to my country, (a commitment absent before the oil billions)—was irresistible to many. Opportunity was there, to do good, and to grow rich in the process. Many of my acquaintances could not resist the new El Dorado, but departures were delayed many months: there was first the lengthy Canadian citizenship process to go through, a process that ended not with a party of celebration but with a quick trip to the passport office.

There is no way to prevent such utilitarianism, and those who wish to acquire only a passport of convenience enjoy the right. (I am reminded of another acquaintance whose wealthy father lives in Hong Kong. When he asked his father why he was not worried about the coming Chinese takeover of the colony, the old man simply opened his desk drawer and directed his gaze in, to a slew of foreign passports, including a Canadian one.) The implications for the country, though, cannot be ignored.

Any country that does not claim the full loyalty of its citizens old or new, any country that embraces citizens old or new who treat it as they would a public washroom—that is, merely as a place to run to in an emergency—accepts for itself a severe internal weakening. It is perhaps inevitable that for many newcomers Canada is merely a job. It is desperately sad, though, when after many years they see Canada as only that; and it is even sadder when their children continue to see Canada with the eyes of foreigners. Multiculturalism, with its emphasis on the importance of holding on to the former or ancestral homeland, with its insistence that *There* is more important than *Here*, serves to encourage such attitudes.

In a democracy, any legislation to address such a problem must be viewed as anathema, for it cannot help but be a gesture of tyranny. So although there is no role here for the legislator, there is a vital role for the policy-maker. Multiculturalism, if it is in fact aimed at shaping Canadian society in a cohesive way, should seek out policies that would encourage engagement with the society rather than exploitation of it.

On the topic of the British-Indian literary community, Salman Rushdie has offered the following warning: "[O]f all the many elephant traps lying ahead of us, the largest and most dangerous pitfall would be the adoption of a ghetto mentality. To forget that there is a world beyond the community to which we belong, to confine ourselves within narrowly defined cultural frontiers, would be, I believe, to go voluntarily into that form of internal exile which in South Africa is called the 'homeland.' We must guard against creating, for the most virtuous of reasons, [...] equivalents of Bophuthatswana or the Transkei."[40]

From this point of view, multiculturalism has served us badly, for it has encouraged us to enter that elephant trap of ethnicity, and to pull the door in securely behind us.

Seven

The Limits of Diversity

In the West Indies, long and boisterous parties, on the whole, inconvenience no one. They are held at houses, both inside and outside. Neighbours tend to be invited; children sleep where they fall. Food and drink are in plentiful supply, music is loud and lively, meant not as background filler but as foreground incentive to dance. There is nothing sedate about the archetypal West Indian party. So central is "a good time" to the West Indian sense of self that someone—not a West Indian—once wryly commented that she had the impression that parties, and not calypso or reggae, were the great West Indian contribution to world culture. Booming music, the yelp and rumble of excited voices, the tramp of dancing feet are accepted as an integral part of the region's cultural life.

Transfer this to, say, Toronto or Vancouver—not to a house surrounded by an extensive yard but to an apartment hemmed in by other apartments. Transfer the music, the dancing, the shouting—everything but the fact that the neighbours, unknown and uncommunicative, are likely to be invited. It takes little imagination to appreciate the tensions that may, and do, arise.

A simple lack of consideration for the rights of others? Yes—but it may be, as some claim, that everything is political. The view has frequently been expressed to me that, in view of the importance of parties in West Indian culture, and considering the official policy of multicultural preservation in Canada, complaints about noise or demands that stereo volumes be lowered can be justifiably viewed as a form of cultural aggression. Changing the tone of the party, the argument goes, results in a lessening of its Caribbean character, and is therefore a sign of cultural intolerance. Implicit in this view is the idea that everything deemed cultural is sacred—as well as the idea that the surrounding society must fully accommodate itself to displays, no matter how disruptive, of cultural life. In this atmosphere, a party is no longer just a party; it becomes a form of cultural expression and therefore under political and legal protection.

This is an admittedly aggressive interpretation of multicultural philosophy, but it is neither far-fetched nor fully indefensible. Open-ended political policy is, almost without exception, subject to an endless stretching of the envelope: there will always be someone—or some group—attempting to go further than anyone else has gone before.

In 1992, the Ontario College of Physicians and Surgeons expressed concern over a rise, unexplained and unexpected, in the number of requests for infibulation, otherwise known as female circumcision. The procedure, long viewed in western culture as a kind of mutilation, involves "cutting off a young girl's external genital parts, including the clitoris. In some countries, it includes stitching closed the vulva until marriage, leaving a small opening for urination and menstrual flow.... Various health risks have been linked to it, including immediate serious bleeding, recurring infections, pain during intercourse, hemorrhaging during childbirth and infertility.... Charles Kayzze, head of Ottawa's African Resource Centre, believes it is being performed here by members of the community. In some cases, he says, families are sending their children to Africa to have it done."[1]

The result is the reduction of the woman to the status of machine, capable of production but mechanically, with no pleasure in the process. This, however, is an unabashedly "Eurocentric" view of infibulation.

A more culturally sensitive view is presented in an article for the *The Globe and Mail*[2] by Christine Hodge, a Canadian working for the United Nations World Food Program in Chad. She tells of a woman named Khadidja Ahmat Rahmasaleh, head of nutritional services in the ministry of social affairs and promotion of the family. Ms. Rahmasaleh, a Muslim, is an intelligent, educated and "forward-thinking" woman dedicated to the traditions of her tribe, her family and her God. But this is not all she is. She has spent five years at university in Italy. She is familiar with the ways of the West, and seeks "to incorporate the ways of two worlds that often seem at loggerheads." Her experiences and studies in Italy convinced her that circumcision "was neither necessary nor right."

And yet, to Ms. Hodge's disappointment, Ms. Rahmasaleh's two daughters, ages seven and nine, decided to undergo the procedure—at the daughters' own request: "Because they were not circumcised, they were not considered to be women. Their friends refused to let them join in games and conversations." Cut off from the life of the community, the girls grew sullen and depressed—and to be cut off from the community in Chad is to risk more than a social life, it is to risk life itself. It was the community that had raised the funds to send Ms. Rahmasaleh to Italy; the community that would provide sustenance in time of inevitable famine; the community that would tend to the children in the event of their mother's death. To leave the girls uncircumcised and, so, alienated from the community, was to sever a vital lifeline.

For any mother, but particularly for a Chadean mother cognizant of her family's uncertain circumstances, it was an intolerable situation. Ms. Rahmasaleh decided the girls would undergo neither of the two traditional procedures—infibulation, in which the entire external genitalia are cut off and the wound sewn up; or the less radical excision of the clitoris and labia major, which would remove sexual pleasure but diminish health risks. She devised instead a method—a pin-prick to the clitoris—that would satisfy the ceremonial need to draw blood while leaving her children intact—unpleasant, no doubt, but not mutilating.

Despite opposition—her own mother and aunts insisted the girls' clitorises be removed—her method, a blending of the old idea with the new, was employed, as it was again later on for her ten-year-old niece.

Ms. Hodge, although not present, was yet able to witness the procedure and the ensuing celebrations through the miracle of technology: everything had been videotaped. She ends her article still opposed to female circumcision—she does not flinch from the word "barbaric"—but with a greater appreciation of the context that prompts its continuance.

And that, in the end, is the point: context is everything. How far, in the Canadian context, do we go in accommodation? Female circumcision is clearly a vital, traditional rite of passage to womanhood for these Chadean women. Do we, in rejecting it, impose an uncontextualized, "Eurocentric" value on certain ethnic groups? Should we, under certain circumstances (a sterile operating room, trained medical personnel), respect the right of certain women to undergo what we see as mutilation? And what of those cultures in which male offspring are vital? Do we permit the use of the available technology to permit sex-selection? But multiculturalism ends where our notions of human rights and dignity begin—and therein lies the thorny question of limits.

The Multiculturalism Act suggests no limits to the accommodation offered to different cultural practices, so that a few years ago a Muslim group in Toronto demanded, in the name of respect for its culture, the right to opt out of the Canadian judicial system in favour of Islamic law, a body of thought fundamental to the life and cultural outlook of its practising members. In the opinion of their spokesmen, this right should be a given in a truly multicultural society. It is not an argument without philosophical merit (on practical grounds, it's a different matter) and one that evokes questions of the larger context: how far can multiculturalism be taken? Can Canada accommodate citizens whose loyalties do not encompass its long-established legal system? It is a sensitive topic.

On January 18, 1994, talk-show host Jane Hawtin of CFRB Radio in Toronto posed the following question: "Should Canada relax its rules and laws to accommodate the Muslim culture?"[3] The question arose from the Montreal case in which a girl had been sodomized by her stepfather and also from a case in Edmonton in which a judge permitted the marriage of a fourteen-year-old pregnant girl. In both cases the judges "cited Muslim values for their leniency." The question—based, as one man said, on "certain preconceived notions about Islam"—prompted protest from some Toronto Muslims. And yet, it is precisely because those "preconceived notions" exist that the question should be asked, the notions debated and cleared up, limits established.

The same could be said about a proposal from a group of women's organizations that sought to overturn a policy that directed police to always lay charges in wife-assault cases.[4] One of the great victories in the battle against violence against women, the policy had come to be seen as inadequate, or even counter-productive, in helping to protect immigrant women and women from visible minorities. The principal reason given for the proposed change was that, because police and the courts seem to deal more harshly with minority groups, assaulted women who call the authorities face ostracization from their own communities. Moreover, "[w]omen, especially from the black community, just simply don't call the police because they are afraid of the consequences for their partner." The answer, the women's groups suggested, was in establishing "tailor-made charging policies by ethnic or racial group, municipality by municipality."

The proposal is one of divisiveness fraught with complexity and rich with racist possibilities. It does not address the inadequacies of the present approach but simply attempts to sidestep them in unwieldy fashion with a show of essentially meaningless cultural and racial sensitivity.

While the acceptance of female circumcision and sex-selection, and the establishment of a separate legal system for Muslims, are virtual impossibilities—they take the right to "opt out" to unacceptable extremes—the racial segregation of schools apparently is not. This is an idea that writer Cecil Foster has described as "sweeping through the Canadian black community. It calls for black-focused public schools, where the curriculum, teachers and emphasis would be primarily black, or 'Afrocentric,' to use the current buzzword."[5]

The drive to segregation is a deep-seated one, prompted by the alienation of black students from the school system. "The textbooks exclude them," Mr. Foster writes, "and the teachers and principals are usually white and uncaring. The entire attitude of the public education system makes them feel set apart by negative stereotypes that black students, for example, are more fulfilled on the basketball court than in the physics lab."

While this view ignores the role of the family—black American novelist Leon Forrest once pointed out that there is "a problem in Afro-American society these days: if a woman has a niece and a nephew, she'll give the niece a copy of a Toni Morrison book and take the nephew to the Bulls game"[6]—the consequence is a dropout rate for black students two or three times higher than for the general student population. It is, by any stretch of the imagination, a worrisome trend, and the temptation to establish schools where a black staff would provide positive role models, "living proof in the classrooms, playgrounds and principals' offices that blacks are capable of achieving great things," must be seductive. Mr. Foster quotes the words of Mr. Vernon Farrell, chairman of the African-Heritage Educators Network: "Black-focused schools will cause students to reflect on shared history, social relationships, belief systems, social practices and collective responses to political and economic realities. Above all, students will develop a sense of identity, critical consciousness and belonging." All the things, in other words, that multiculturalism was supposed to provide and has not.

This construction of a safer world, the withdrawal into it, is a sign of despair. It indicates dissatisfactions with the world as it is and a lack of faith that the system can ever acquire legitimacy. The despair is not difficult to understand. It comes from the evisceration that follows years of anger and fatigue—both of which emerge from living constantly with society's stereotypical brushings. A black youth commits a crime and all black youths must suffer the suspicion of the streets: the wary eyes, the tensed bodies, the wide berths. How many people react in similar fashion to white or Asian youths in the aftermath of a crime committed by one of their number? As educator and activist Lennox Farrell wrote in a letter to *The Globe and Mail* following the murder of Georgina Leimonis in a Toronto restaurant, "I must...mourn for the collective loss of innocence experienced by some young men who, wherever they go, get the stare, the attitude, the comments from total strangers, simply because they look like other young men involved in criminal activities; other young men who are black."[7] The dream of flight, of retreat, is a plea for security, an urge that is understandable but also, by its very nature, self-defeating, even when it is presented as principle, clothed in buzzwords.

Buzzwords are dangerous creatures. They disguise with quasi-intellectual terminology the true nature of the topic they pretend to describe; they lend a respectability, an apparent complexity, to essentially simplistic ideas. An "Afrocentric" or "black-focused" school system, racially segregated, racially staffed, would simply be a return to the past: to the racial separations of the American south; to the separate but (un)equal approaches of apartheid. It might produce higher grades—and even that is debatable[8]—but would it prepare students for the wider world? It might facilitate the acquisition of knowledge, but would it facilitate the socialization necessary to life beyond the comforting confines of its walls?

A separate education system is an illusory answer to the problems faced by black youth in our society. It would solve nothing, and when students graduate they would inevitably feel the falling away of its racial comforts. It would merely provide a context for withdrawal from society, while the problems—racial and otherwise—can be solved only by engagement with it. It is, in the end, as Mr. Foster points out, simply a recipe for self-ghettoization.

Unlike infibulation and sex-selection, a racially segregated school system is a topic of serious and prolonged discussion. It is an idea that, to many, has great merit. It is not to me. Racial segregation has never been a pretty thing; it has betrayed more than it has aided. Moreover, if we give black parents the right to send their children to all-black schools, do we also give the right to white parents to send their children to all-white schools? And does not such an approach spell the death of any ideal of a multi-racial, multi-ethnic society?

One does not surrender to problems; one grapples with them. Problems exist in the public school system; the needs of many of its students are not being met. It is in that arena, then, and not in the artificial creation of a separate one, that the solutions must be found.

Because we have failed to establish the limits of diversity, because we have so blithely accepted the mentality of division, we find ourselves lost in a confusion of values. Multiculturalism has made us fearful of defining acceptable boundaries; it has caused us to confuse the establishment of circumscription with a lack of respect. And so we find ourselves in danger of accepting, in its name, a slide into ethical chaos. We say no to voluntary infibulation, but consider saying yes to voluntary racial segregation.

How selectively, in our confusion, we judge our evils.

Personal disruptiveness, female circumcision, a separate legal system, racial segregation: it may seem that I am here compiling a catalogue of the worst aspects of multiculturalism. And so, I suppose, I am. None of these excesses in itself constitutes an indictment, but taken together they illustrate the psychology of divisiveness without limits. Excesses cannot be denied; they too are part of the fabric and must be reckoned with. Together they pose the question of how far we, or any society, can go in accommodating diversity. It is the excesses, of demand or of action, that push the boundaries; they challenge basic notions in ways uncomfortable but necessary. The difficulty is in gauging the validity of excess—but to gauge one must first have a sense of one's own beliefs, one's own limits.

There is a logic to these excesses. It is a logic indicative of a certain disdain for the legal and ethical values that shape, and are shaped by, Canadian society—and therefore for Canadian society itself. And why should this not be so, given that the picture the country transmits of itself is one that appears to diminish a unified whole in favour of an ever-fraying mosaic? There may be more communities in the "community of communities" than former prime minister Joe Clark suspects, or is prepared to contend with.

If Canada, as an historical, social, legal and cultural concept, does not demand respect for itself and its ideals, why should any respect be expected?

Eight

Diversity and Creativity

Art is a passion of the mind. And the imagination works best when it is most free. Western writers have always felt free to be eclectic in their selection of theme, setting, form; Western visual artists have, in this century, been happily raiding the visual storehouses of Africa, Asia, the Philippines. I am sure that we must grant ourselves an equal freedom.

Salman Rushdie
"Imaginary Homelands"[1]

How easy it is, in life and in art, to give and to take offence.

The language is littered with the corpses of unworthy terminology: the mentally or physically handicapped are now the mentally or physically challenged; AIDS victims have become People with AIDS (suggesting that we must now talk of People with Accidents); failures are now defined as incomplete successes, and companies no longer fire or lay off people, they downsize and destaff. U.S. real-estate advertisers are now advised to avoid red-light words such as "executive" (which could be racist, since most corporate executives are white), "master bedroom" (which could be suggestive of slavery), "walk-in closet" (which might offend those who cannot walk) and "spectacular view" (which might offend those who cannot see).

And a Canadian publisher, Douglas Gibson of McClelland & Stewart Ltd., relishes the following story: In a speech to an industry convention, Mr. Gibson, a clever and witty man, attacked the federal government's tax on books by saying, "Those who tax reading must be people who find reading taxing." The line was greeted with laughter and applause. But afterward, one person approached him to register displeasure. "That was a clever line," the man said. "Many people laughed. I did not. I'm dyslexic. It's not nice to imply that people who have a hard time reading are stupid."

It is a particularly perilous time for those who work with words. Speech and copy writers, journalists, academics and novelists must exercise greater than usual caution in the selection of their words. Even if, for the writer, a word such as "candle" means simply a stick of wax used to provide illumination, it will be taken by many to mean much more than it says, so that, for instance, if a power outage in a novel should prompt a male character to offer a candle to a female character, his action may be interpreted as a form of sexual aggression. It is one consequence of literature courses around the world that teach students to seek significance in every word, comma and period. There is little scope for essays and dissertations, after all, if a candle is just a candle. A candle must be more than itself if it is to bear the weight of ideology.

In her short story "Labour Day Dinner," Alice Munro writes: "Ruth is wearing a white shirt belonging to her brother, his striped pyjama bottoms, and a monumental black turban. She looks like a proud but good-natured Sikh."[2]

Proud *but* good-natured?

The harmless conjunction could, if one so wished, unleash a torrent of ill-feeling, for it could be construed as implying that proud Sikhs are not on the whole good-natured; it could be taken as indicative of distrust of Sikh pride—indeed, distrust of any minority group with a sense of self.

But to read all of this into the innocent conjunction, to suspect Ms. Munro of harbouring hostilities, one must be prey to particularly febrile sensitivities. One must be governed by a sense of historical and ethnic injustice married to a refusal to understand or forgive. One must be able to see behind that "but" a mental convergence between Ms. Munro and those who mistreated the passengers of the *Komagata Maru* in 1914. One must be in love, then, with one's own victimhood. Sikhs, happily, have far greater problems to worry about, and they are a people on the whole too proud to be silly. Unfortunately, such silliness—the obsessive desire to seek offence and the obsessive desire to avoid giving it—are rampant elsewhere, sprouting vigorously in the upturned soil of the multicultural land.

Sometimes, the twists and turns of sensitivities being unpredictable, even the greatest of care is insufficient. Inoffensiveness can never be taken for granted.

Consider, for instance, "The Hockey Sweater," Roch Carrier's classic story of life in a small Quebec town in the late forties. It is a simple and effective tale that depicts, through the neatly captured voice of a child, a life governed by the imperatives of school, church and hockey:

> The winters of my childhood were long, long, seasons. We lived in three places—the school,

> the church and the skating rink—but our real life was on the skating-rink.... [S]chool was...a quiet place where we could prepare for the next hockey game, lay out our next strategies. As for church, we found there the tranquility of God: there we forgot school and dreamed about the next hockey game. Through our day-dreams it might happen that we would recite a prayer: we would ask God to help us play as well as Maurice Richard.[3]

When the boy—who, like his friends, worships the Montreal Canadiens—outgrows his Canadiens hockey sweater, his mother orders a new one from the Eaton's mail-order department. The store mistakenly supplies a Toronto Maple Leafs sweater. Forced to wear it because his mother fears offending Monsieur Eaton, an *anglais*, the boy's anger flares on the ice after he is given what he considers an unfair penalty. He smashes his stick in frustration, only to be confronted by the young vicar:

> "My child," he said, "just because you're wearing a new Toronto Maple Leafs sweater unlike the others, it doesn't mean you're going to make the laws around here. A proper young man doesn't lose his temper. Now take off your skates and go to the church and ask God to forgive you."
>
> Wearing my Maple Leafs sweater I went to the church, where I prayed to God; I asked him to send, as quickly as possible, moths that would eat up my Toronto Maple Leafs sweater.

"The Hockey Sweater" is a charming story that reveals much about the sporting and religious life of Quebec as well as, more generally, about the mythology of hockey in Canada. It speaks to many, even to those not enamoured of hockey. One would not expect it to upset anyone.

But it may be that expectations exist in order to be demolished.

Some years after its initial appearance, the publishers received a letter requesting permission to include the story in a new anthology for schools. The letter requested "some minor changes" in view of the fact that the anthology would be used "by elementary students from varying backgrounds and religions"; specifically, it requested the deletion of all references to God and was accompanied by photocopies of the relevant pages with the offending words scratched out.

More recently, the novelist Alberto Manguel wrote of his own experience with an offending word.[4] Invited to contribute to the introduction of a book on the immigrant experience, he wrote that "Canada has been perceived as a land of noble savages..." To his consternation, the word "savages" was taken out and replaced by the word "natives." This was done at the insistence of the publisher's native liaison officer, "who considered the use of the word 'savage' unacceptable 'in any context.'" He or she was apparently unfamiliar with the eighteenth-century literary concept of the noble savage, to which Mr. Manguel was referring. "To change the wording," Mr. Manguel points out, "to prettify the concept by replacing 'savage' with 'native' is an arrogant attempt to modify history.... Language is inextricable from the society that uses it; we are defined by our vocabulary, by the words we used and by the words we use."

Censorship is nothing new in this world. It appears everywhere in one guise or another, for reasons that are not always ill-meaning but are nearly always misguided.

William Shakespeare's *The Merchant of Venice* is a particular favourite of the censors. While Shylock's portrayed viciousness is seen as the product of anti-Semitism, his moving plea for recognition of his humanity remains largely ignored. I was only ten or eleven when I first read the play (for a primary school production that never materialized), and from the beginning the portrait of Shylock struck me as moving and complex, a compelling reminder that even though human beings may be turned into brutes by circumstance and experience, they remain human beings. This is an unsettling truth, for it challenges the satisfying prejudices we all harbour. We do not have to like or even forgive the brutes among us, but we ignore their humanity at our own peril.

And yet the play has caused problems in classrooms. As Bernie M. Farber, national director for community relations for the Canadian Jewish Congress, has written, Shylock's redeeming qualities are of no importance "to the 14-year-old Jewish student who, after viewing a production of *The Merchant of Venice* a few months ago, had pennies and gum wrappers pelted at him by other students. And it makes little difference to the dozens of Jewish students who have been referred to as 'Jewish dog,' 'Jew devil' and 'Shylock,' or have had swastikas carved in their desks or coins thrown at them as a result of youthful insensitivities following the play's reading in class."[5]

Such actions would suggest, though, that the problem is not with the play but with the way in which it is presented. Shylock, properly explored, would not bring taunts to Jewish students but a new sympathy, a recognition of the viciousness to which Jews[6] have historically been subjected. No better vehicle exists for an exploration of anti-Semitism. The Canadian Jewish Congress, as Mr. Farber makes clear, does not call for the banning of the play, as others have done, but does insist that its full context be explored, its perspectives on prejudice and bigotry stressed.

This is the only sensible approach to controversial works, but it requires a basic trust in the instincts and intelligence of teachers and students. It requires a trust that free people can think for themselves, can examine different points of view and, with appropriate guidance, come to appropriate conclusions.

This is not a trust that Mr. Victor Doerksen, a Conservative member of the Alberta legislature, is prepared to extend. In March 1994, during national Freedom to Read Week (the irony would, in all likelihood, have been lost on the Honorable Member), he delivered an eight-hundred-name petition to the legislature demanding that John Steinbeck's *Of Mice and Men* be banned from all Alberta school libraries. The petition called on the government "not to allow literature in the education system that is intolerant of any religion, including Christianity, or demeans or profanes the name of God and Jesus Christ."[7] Although admitting he has not read the 118-page novel, Mr. Doerksen nevertheless insisted that it uses "profane words" 198 times. (The thought does occur to me that Mr. Doerksen may in fact be doing the students a favour. Banning the book may be the one infallible way to ensure that they read it—surreptitiously, without guidance, seeking out only the titillating or "offensive" parts ...)

John Steinbeck is not the only Nobel prize winner to merit such treatment from people like Mr. Doerksen, though. The use of the word "fuck," so shocking to students' sensibilities, has prompted calls for the banning of Aleksandr Solzhenitsyn's *One Day in the Life of Ivan*

Denisovich; as has the use of the word "nigger" in William Golding's *Lord of the Flies*, Harper Lee's *To Kill a Mockingbird* and Mark Twain's *Huckleberry Finn*. Closer to home, the sexuality in Margaret Laurence's *The Diviners* frequently proves too offensive to bear, as do W. P. Kinsella's depictions of natives.

Of course, we have never been a country entirely devoted to the idea of freedom of speech. Once Mr. Doerksen's political career is over, he can always seek employment among the ranks of the literary critics hired by Canada Customs to protect us from the literary depravities flooding in from abroad, all those books that promote "a homosexual lifestyle" (whatever that is), debase the family and demean Christian values, books that just might contravene our hate laws, such as Salman Rushdie's *The Satanic Verses*, which was "delayed" by Customs so that its critics could judge the work's literary merits.

In this atmosphere, even the warnings of the past must be handled with care, as Reform Party MP for Okanagan Centre Werner Schmidt found out when his constituency newsletter quoted Adolf Hitler: "What luck for rulers that men do not think."[8] The resulting furore—the Canadian Jewish Congress condemned the use of a mass-murderer's words in an MP's newsletter as "highly offensive" and "inexcusable"—led to quick apologies from party leader Preston Manning and an extraordinary statement from a chastened Mr. Schmidt: "I would never have put it in there personally because I don't think a person who has such an odious history or background should ever be quoted."[9] Any use of Hitler's name or words is bound to be controversial, but do we not do ourselves a disservice by refusing ever to quote him? The lessons to be drawn from a life like Hitler's are many and varied. Ugliness, like beauty, has much to impart.

In the face of these cases, and of hundreds like them, the request to delete God from "The Hockey Sweater" seems minor. But the attitude implicit in the request—that literature must be shaped and sanitized in order to avoid all possibility of giving offence—is now making itself felt in ways that are exquisitely mind-boggling for writers. Many gods other than He of the Old and New Testaments have been erected: ethnic gods, gender gods. They all have their defenders. They all claim their victims.

To write a book, have it published and sent out into the world is to engage a public life, with all of its thrills and all of its perils. It is to take the fancies of deeply private moments and offer them for the amusement, the scrutiny, the elucidation of others. The grandest thrill is to discover that others, friends and strangers alike, find a certain value in what you have to say. The greatest peril is to find thrust upon you expectations never anticipated during those long hours of making sentences, expectations which more often than not take the form of roles one is expected to play, attitudes one is expected to adopt.

My first book, a collection of short stories entitled *Digging Up the Mountains*, was published in 1985. I submitted myself to a round of media interviews, among them one with a man who said he was a journalist from Trinidad. We had a long chat over coffee, but it became clear as we spoke that he had not taken the trouble to read my book, a not unusual occurrence. Some days later, after the publication of an interview I had done with a writer from *NOW* magazine, I received a phone call from this man. His first words to me were, "Neil, I'm disappointed in you." How so? I asked. He explained that I had written and said things that I should not have about corruption and racism and the dangers of life in the Caribbean. I realized then that he'd read the book as well as the *NOW* interview.

We talked for forty-five minutes, during which time he admitted that he agreed with all I had said—but, really, I should not be saying it here, in Canada. I finally brought the conversation to an end when I realized that we had irreconcilable views on the role of the writer: while I sought to reflect reality as faithfully as I could in my writing, he expected me to play the role of propagandist for the tourist industry back in the islands. Why write about corruption when there were sandy beaches to describe? Why write about racism when Carnival was so much more colourful? I had let "my people" down. I was pointing to the shadows when he wanted the sun.

Writer as propagandist, writer as salesperson, writer as spokesperson. The world offers a dizzying array of extra-literary possibilities for the writer—all of them attractive, all of them perilous.

For writers "of colour" (a group that apparently includes every hue but the pinkish), the political and racial expectations of others can prove particularly onerous. This was brought home to me early in my career when, some months after the publication of that first book, a magazine called *Fuse* published a piece by a woman named Marlene Philip.

Ostensibly a review of my book, the title said it all: "Naipaul's Legacies: Continuing the Colonizers' Dirty Work." Ms. Philip, a Toronto writer and social commentator, took me to task on several counts. Not only did I overwrite, she stated, but I suffered from an "arrant refusal to contextualize" my characters, engaging in an "utter, absolute and deliberate dehistoricization of everything and everyone" of which I wrote (this she kindly blamed on my youth). In my writing she also perceived that "people's blackness, be it hair or facial features, become reason for criticism or ridicule," making me racist. In addition to which I was politically suspect: not only did I "pimp the tawdry racist views of colonial powers, past and present, the world over" (quite an achievement, it seemed to me, for a first book of short stories), but "a reference to Marx and Castro is within a decidedly negative context—to reflect unwelcome change—and is entirely unbalanced by any reference to American imperialism in the Caribbean."

With the publication of my second book in 1988, a novel entitled *A Casual Brutality*, Ms. Philip again fired up her word-processor in response to my "Immoral Fiction."[10] The usual accusations are trotted out—the colonial vision, the racist mind, the dehistoricization—and others are added: misogyny, social amnesia, the immorality of "a writer shitting on his country of birth." And so, with this final accusation, we come around to the equivalent of *Neil, I'm disappointed in you*, to criticism not literary but political. In another piece, she issues her blanket condemnation: "Authors like V. S. Naipaul and his nephew Neil Bissoondath are both examples of writers who catapulted to fame on the savage and, at times, racist critique of the 'Third World.'"[11]

If I dwell on Ms. Philip's criticism of my work, it is not for simply personal motives. I have little interest in responding to diatribe; engaging in polemic with ideologues is pointless and tiresome. For those who covet it, ideological vision is like religion: there is no challenging them, they are true believers in the deepest sense of the term. But Ms. Philip, under the new name of M. Nourbese Philip, has since gone on to greater things, and her criticism of me and my work is simply part of a larger pattern that bears further scrutiny. If William Gairdner is a popular spokesman for the political, racial right, then

Ms. Philip is in many ways a (somewhat less) popular spokesperson for the political, racial left.

We have, in this country, accepted with little hesitation the psychology of separation. We have, through the practice of multiculturalism, created a kind of psychic apartheid, the "homelands of the mind" Salman Rushdie has warned us about. As our provinces, greedy for power, pull apart, so too do our communities, greedy for "rights," pull apart. Once the psychology of separation takes hold, no logical limits suggest themselves, so that we go on, as a country, as a people, seeking to narrow ourselves in every way possible and in many ways unimaginable, retreating behind the barricades of self-imposed ghettos. This is an insidious psychology. Once the institutional division of people by culture is accepted, it becomes easy to subdivide them in other ways too—by gender, for example, or by race.

In the fall of 1989, Marlene Philip gained brief notoriety as the woman June Callwood publicly (and, by her own admission, not uncharacteristically)[12] told to fuck off.

Callwood's version of the incident is straightforward: On the evening of September 24, 1989, as she was leaving a gala concert for PEN International at Roy Thomson Hall in Toronto, she was accosted by demonstrators alleging racism in Canadian artistic circles in general and in the composition of the Canadian PEN contingent in particular. Among the protesters was Marlene Philip, who attempted to give a leaflet to Callwood. "I said fuck off," Callwood told Adele Freedman. "It seemed bizarre behaviour, so I said fuck off and went on my way."

Ms. Philip, who has written that she always attempts "to disturb the peace of those invested in maintaining the status quo,"[13] has a slightly different recollection. The leafletting was "small, low-keyed"; no one was accosted. If there was any abuse, it was by June Callwood, who uttered the two-word phrase three times in an "unprovoked and unwarranted" attack.

Ms. Callwood's irritation and Ms. Philip's dismay are equally understandable, and it is impossible to say, from this distance, whether or not there was provocation. What is certain, though, is that, having directed the epithet at a black woman, June Callwood has come to be haunted by accusations of racism. The price has been heavy. Despite her impeccable record of social activism, Ms. Callwood has been hounded from the board of Nellie's, a women's hostel she helped found, and from the Writers' Union of Canada, of which she was also a founding member.

Ms. Callwood's fate brings to mind that of Jeanne Cannizzo, a one-time anthropology professor at the University of Toronto who some years ago curated an exhibition called "Into the Heart of Africa," about African art and Canadian missionaries, for the Royal Ontario Museum. It wasn't long before some black groups denounced the exhibition and its curator as racist and began picketing the ROM. The ensuing controversy proved devastating to Ms. Cannizzo. "Enemies of her exhibition wrote racist graffitti on her house," Robert Fulford wrote, "invaded her classroom, shouted her down, and threatened physical harm. She withdrew from teaching and fell silent."[14] She has since left the country.

The controversy prompted a startlingly revealing essay by Susan Crean, a writer, art critic and, in one pithy description, "observer of Canadian culture." Ms. Crean's view is summed up in the clever, if not terribly subtle, title, "Taking the Missionary Position."[15] Her piece is not favourable to the exhibition. "Cannizzo," she writes, "creates a context in which [the history of Canadian missionaries in Africa] is claimed rather than criticized and rejected." That history can be *rejected* is a peculiar point of view. That it should be the purpose of a museum exhibition to reject history goes beyond peculiar to mind-boggling.

Ms. Crean then takes exception to Ms. Cannizzo's historical contextualizing, which explains "Great Uncle" (the Canadian missionary in Africa) as a product of his time. But are we not all the products of our time? It was Great Uncle's role to preach and pillage, as it is Susan Crean's to blush and atone: his times made him, as her times make her. Ms. Crean also points out that Ms. Cannizzo puts ironic quotes around such phrases as "barbarous people" and "savage customs"—but "such subtle irony," she comments, "is not only lost on those who can't (or don't) read the explanatory texts, it is also a pretty limp way to examine a subject as grave as racially motivated genocide." What Ms. Crean is in fact saying here is that, first, Ms. Cannizzo is responsible for the reactions of those who do not view the totality of the exhibit, and, second, that only intellectuals who understand such things as "ironic quotes" can have the subtlety of mind to understand the message. Ms. Cannizzo, then, is not as frank and direct as Ms. Crean thinks she ought to be. And yet a wall-sized sketch of a mounted British soldier plunging his sword into the chest of a Zulu warrior—no more vivid and unvarnished an image of the evils perpetrated by imperialism can be imagined—prompts Ms. Crean to accuse Ms. Cannizzo of "weird disregard for the sensibilities of visitors, especially black children."

Jeanne Cannizzo could have won only if her explanatory texts had read something like, "See the evil white man mistreating the noble natives ..."

There is more than a hint of condescension in all of this, the condescension of the guilt-ridden intellectual hastening to prove herself more sensitive to racial issues than people of colour, more ethnic than the ethnics. The article, in the end, reveals the confusion often found in white left-liberal circles: not the exercise of intellect but the abdication of it, not exploration of ideas but conversation in a confessional.

In a collection of essays entitled *Frontiers* Ms. Philip deals with the issues surrounding both June Callwood and Jeanne Cannizzo. In each she finds an embedded racism—as she does in the Canada Council, the Ontario Arts Council, the Toronto Arts Council, the Toronto police force and the justice system, the publishing industry and book-reviewing circles, TVOntario and the media as a whole, in American novelist Alice Walker's *The Color Purple* and its awarding of the Pulitzer prize. It is a formidable list. A sense emerges from a reading of her book of being under siege, of living in a society in which a vigorous racist conspiracy continually rebuffs the attempts of people of colour to find a place.

Ms. Philip's is not an isolated view. It is one shared by a variety of Canadians from a variety of backgrounds. Professor Roy Miki, a Canadian of Japanese descent, is also chair of the Writers' Union of Canada's Racial Minority Writers' Committee, which organized "Writing Thru [sic] Race," a Conference for First Nations writers and writers of colour in Vancouver. The aim of the conference, as described in the information sheet, is to allow First Nations writers and writers of colour "to address the impact of 'race' and racism in contemporary writing in Canada." In order to achieve this goal, the following conference policy was announced: "To ensure a milieu in which writers directly affected by racism can engage in candid and personal discussions, enrolment in the conference will include only First Nations writers and writers of colour. The evening literary events are open to the general public." The question of how much colour a writer of colour should have in order to qualify for enrolment was not addressed.

In a lengthy essay of justification in the Union's newletter, Union chair Myrna Kostash detailed her slow and difficult conversion to the idea of a racially exclusive conference. Her defence of white participation turned around on what struck her as the single compelling point: "[I]t was the *need* to talk among themselves as writers of colour on issues of compelling importance *without having to worry all the time about how we whites are feeling*" (her italics).[16] What, one wonders, would writers of colour say amongst themselves that they would not dare say in the presence of whites? The charges of racism, publicly, repeatedly and tearfully stated by First Nations writers such as Lee Maracle and Lenore Keeshig-Tobias, have not been noticeably reticent.

Ms. Kostash was further persuaded that "writers of colour were *respecting* white writers enough to assume that we will understand why they need to meet alone."

It may seem to some that Ms. Kostash is easily persuaded, but the arguments are calculated to manipulate: if you do not let us meet alone, the first suggests, you are revealing an unkind distrust of us; if we respect you enough to exclude you, the second suggests, then you should respect us enough to accept exclusion. To argue against such logic is to expose oneself to charges of racism. Ms. Kostash can be forgiven for allowing herself to be persuaded to see "Writing Thru Race" as representing "intellectual and literary enrichment." And yet, how curious it is that people who seek inclusion despite their colour would choose to be exclusive because of it.

The debate both within the Writers' Union and in the media has been vigorous. It began with Robert Fulford in *The Globe and Mail* lamenting the move from pluralism, with its emphasis on the rights of the individual, to multiculturalism, with its emphasis on the rights of the group, promoting the vision "of each of us as the member of a racially designated cluster."[17] Mr. Fulford saw justification of the whites-excluded conference as indicating that "closed is open, limited is free, exclusion is inclusion, and private is public."

Soon the debate was publicly engaged. Roy Miki, responding in the *Globe*,[18] began by labelling Mr. Fulford's article an April Fool's trick. "The kind of pluralism Mr. Fulford yearns for," he wrote, "is really the resurrected form of an earlier assimilationist ideology that was used historically to promote Anglo-European values and traditions as the Canadian norm." After outlining a history of Canadian racism, he offered the opinion that one consequence of assimilation was that "writers whose work did not conform to mainstream Anglo-European assumptions were not taken seriously," making it difficult for "First Nations writers and writers of colour to communicate across their own cultures, languages." A truly pluralistic society, he continues, "would encourage those who have been harmed by racism to work together to find ways of eliminating its negative effects"—which is undoubtedly true, but fails to address the question of why a conference devoted to fighting the effects of racism should itself indulge in a kind of racism. Once more, too, there is the upended logic of manipulation: if you oppose this conference, you do not believe in a truly pluralistic society.

On May 9, 1994, again in the *Globe*, Myrna Kostash returned to the fray. Like Mr. Miki, she offered an example of historical Canadian racism—at the beginning of the century her highly educated Ukrainian uncle was not considered "white" enough for the post of weed inspector in Alberta—and, after criticizing Mr. Fulford and

Michael Valpy for their opposition to the conference, she cast its critics as people fearful of change, resentful of "having to learn a new vocabulary, their dawning awareness that the content of Canadianness is no longer just white or 'wannabe' white.... In 'whiteness,' they feel, was wholeness; in ethnic and racial diversity are fragmentation and antagonism." In other words, racism. It is a simplification, even a misrepresentation, of the expressed opposition, but it also indicates clearly the approach taken by conference supporters, an approach reminiscent of a claim I once heard that if a situation is deemed racist by a person of colour, it must be accepted as such by everyone else, and any argument to the contrary is itself indicative of racism. Ms. Kostash is right in arguing for a greater inclusiveness, but it seems contradictory to argue that a further exercise in racial divisiveness is a way to achieve that goal.

The actual holding of this conference is immaterial: it will change nothing. Of greater interest is the thinking—the "philosophy" and the context—behind the stated policy.

In a column supportive of the conference, Bronwyn Drainie quotes Mr. Miki's explanation of why, despite its best efforts, one of the country's top journalism schools has been unsuccessful in recruiting students from non-white minorities: "It's because we are so afraid of entering the language-based professions. Why do you think so many Asian students gravitate towards math, science and engineering? It is very threatening not just to work in English, but to work in it *well.*"[19] Mr. Miki then went on to speak of his parents' terror when he decided to study English literature: "They were convinced it was a dead end, that I would never be accepted as a university teacher. And certainly, when I was doing my graduate studies at Simon Fraser and UBC, there were no other students of colour in the graduate English departments at all." It is a picture of loneliness—of the young man bravely entering an unfamiliar, intimidating and vaguely menacing world. As such it is similar to V.S. Naipaul's portraits of the racial insecurity of a brown man in a white England in the fifties: the sense of isolation, of aloneness, in a strange and perhaps unwelcoming land. But whereas Mr. Naipaul casts his experience in personal terms, Mr. Miki casts his in political and racial ones. Whereas loneliness has led Mr. Naipaul to an unassailable individuality, it has led Mr. Miki to a sense of community he has described as "racialized."

Perhaps I reveal my naïvety—or simply my distance from racial concepts and politics—in admitting that "racialized" was a fairly new word to me. I first saw it in a piece by poet and short-story writer Dionne Brand in *Brick* magazine, in which she offers me, by name, the rather obscure warning that Eurocentric, racist, sexist "discourses seep into places, corners" where I live in my "'racialized' self." I can only assume this to be a poetic way of saying that I, as a brown-skinned man, am also affected by racism—which is hardly news to someone who grew up with the racial antagonisms of Trinidad.

"Racialized" popped up again in Roy Miki's explanation of the conference: where he admits that "some writers, particularly those not racialized as 'of colour,' may be tempted to critique this policy as exclusionary and separatist."

Racialized as "of colour": the term seems to imply a sense of one's own race within an appreciation of the larger racial context, the ability, in other words, to see life and all its ramifications through the colour of one's own skin. If this definition is fair, I must plead guilty to not being racialized.

For to be racialized, it seems to me, is to adopt a narrowed vision of life. It is to seek positive change from the racial approach that produced *Mein Kampf* and apartheid. It cannot be benign. Can the racial pride of a Jean-Marie Le Pen be distinguished from that of a Louis Farrakhan, and is it possible to find a middle ground?

As Robert Fulford has pointed out, a sense of victimization seems to be an intimate part of racialization:

> Miki describes himself as Japanese-Canadian, "an identity historically produced through the conjunction of Anglo-European racism and the will to resist erasure." That passage in itself deserves careful reading, since it neatly encapsulates, in under 20 words, the radically conflicting messages of multiculturalism. It says that racism helped create his identity, and that Japanese-Canadians have resisted "erasure" by maintaining their ethnicity. It seems to say that if whites single out Japanese-Canadians as different, then that's racism; but if whites insist that race doesn't matter, and treat a Japanese-Canadian as they treat everyone else, then that's also a bad thing, because it could erase Miki's identity. Miki manages to position himself simultaneously as a victim and a proud Japanese-Canadian.[20]

To be a victim of the past is to be burdened by the sense that history—colonialism, imperialism, racism, sexism—has victimized you, and this sense of historical injustice has become a full and active element of your personality. You are informed by more than just the memory of it; it impels you to view the world in a certain way, to act in a certain way; it hardens you, makes you combative: you claim the moral high-ground and live to see your victimhood acknowledged and compensated. But to chain yourself to the injustices and humiliations of the past is to march forward into the future with your gaze fixed firmly behind you.

The culture of victimhood is composed of conceit and theatre, the threads of which stitch themselves through the ideas of multiculturalism. "Writing Thru Race" is a conference for and by writers who feel they have not enjoyed the success they believe they deserve—a success that has been denied them not by a paucity of talent or a lack of hard work but by simple racism. If their works have not been published, or if they have been badly published or badly reviewed, the fault lies with racism, systemic or personal. And yet, the difficulties of getting published, and published effectively—with good production, good distribution, wide notices—is one shared by every writer and would-be writer in the country, regardless of colour or ethnicity. If many First Nations writers and writers of colour have been ill-served by the publishing industry, so too have many white writers. There is much good writing being produced, and there is even more bad writing. Publishers will not turn down the chance to make money. They do their best to seek out and promote good work, but they too are human, with all the failings of other humans. It is at best ungenerous to label their fallibility as racism, or to accuse them of tokenism when they try to draw attention to their track record in publishing "minority" writers and their plans for future projects. At what point, it must be asked, does tokenism stop being tokenism? How many "minority" writers must be published before the accusation is retired? Moreover, does the publication of work at great expense and effort not because it is good but in order to equalize racial statistics not constitute the very definition of institutionalized tokenism?

But, of course, the argument is defeated by the insistence that publishers are all Eurocentric, and so incapable of appreciating writing that is not ...

History and its wrongs make up one of the pillars of racialization and the racialized self. Nasty things happened years ago in Canada. But that is a Canada that no longer exists. The world is no longer what it was. A host of writers in many countries have followed in the footsteps of V. S. Naipaul; graduate English departments are chock-full of colours; and in the world of Canadian literary criticism, the late Ken Adachi, like Mr. Miki of Japanese descent, ranks with the very best.

This has not been an edifying debate. Throughout the mud-slinging and the name-calling and the self-pity, one could hear the background swish of the whips of self-flagellation peeling the skin from white backs. These have been the defining tones of much of the multicultural debate.

Racialization seeks to co-opt racism, to deny its sting by embracing it, but racism is an unstable companion. If racialization is a qualification for participation in "Writing Thru Race," as it is more and more for defining oneself as "ethnic" and thus a participant in multiculturalism, there is reason to worry. Mr. Miki hopes for a future in which race "and racialization will have become obsolete as technologies of control and definition," but racialization today cannot lead to a world where race does not matter tomorrow. On the contrary, it can mean only a world where race matters *in every way.*

In the end, the national council of the Writers' Union of Canada, at its annual general meeting in May 1994, proposed a resolution stating "that while the union is committed to 'greater racial minority access within writing and publishing' and reaffirmed its support for the forthcoming conference, it also recognized the rights of all members to be involved in union business they feel affects them. Therefore, 'in future, [we] will adhere to the principle that the union officially sponsor only those activities that are open to all union members.'"[21] After wide-ranging debate, the motion was tabled until next year's annual general meeting. The decision was...not to make a decision. The Writers' Union of Canada had exorcised courage from its convictions.

Appropriation of Voice

The urge to segregate first made itself felt in the Canadian literary community in 1987 when a nasty spat developed among the editors of the Women's Press in Toronto. A proposed short-story anthology ran into trouble when objections were raised, in part by Marlene Philip,[22] concerning certain of the stories already contracted for publication. The problem was simple: white female writers had written from the viewpoint of black female characters; they had "appropriated" the experiences of women already exploited in a society dominated by white males. The white writers had, in telling the stories of black women, practised a kind of cultural imperialism. The house, a vital and necessary publisher, split viciously over the issue. A kind of in-house coup ensued. Locks were changed, jobs were lost.

But this was just the beginning. Soon other demands were made: not only must whites not write about blacks, but men must not write about women, non-natives about natives, and so on, all based on the claim that if you haven't lived the life, you don't have the right to write about it. And the writer who dares to explore the territory deemed not his or her own becomes a thief, open to charges of racism, sexism, imperialism from people who object to being portrayed in ways other than they would portray themselves—and self-portraits, let us face it, tend to be free of blemishes.

Fields other than writing have also felt the cultural appropriation sting. In 1992, Montreal painter Lyne Robichaud entered a painting called "Woman with Bananas" in an exhibition of work by Concordia University student artists. The painting, a portrait of a black woman carrying a bunch of bananas on her head, reflected a certain dignity in the midst of hardship. It was, if anything, deeply sympathetic. But Lyne Robichaud soon found her work removed from exhibition after a committee ruled her work racist: Lyne Robichaud was white, her subject black. Protests were to no avail, and the public was treated to the delicious spectacle of a committee of self-righteous white women protecting the dignity of black women by censoring a moving portrait by a white woman.

In an article in *Brick* magazine, writer Dionne Brand accuses my portrayals of women and blacks of simply revalidating the myths of "Eurocentric discourse," of drawing "only the stereotype so helpful in white domination," of filtering their voices "through the Eurocentric screen of racist, sexist discourse." Further, "[i]n producing a Neil Bissoondath to denounce the cultural appropriation critique, the white cultural establishment produces a dark face to dismiss and discredit all the other dark faces and simultaneously to confirm and reinscribe that colonial representation which is essential to racial domination."[23]

There is no doubt that to accept the tenets of cultural appropriation is to condemn me. I have written not only from the viewpoint of young, brown-skinned men of East Indian descent born in the Caribbean and living in Canada but also from the perspectives of a young Japanese woman, young black men and young black women, a young central American girl, a middle-aged Spanish man and an elderly Jewish man, a young white woman and a young white man, a Marxist revolutionary and a CIA agent. I have written about the left and the right and their victims. I have written about political oppressors and the politically oppressed.

Little wonder, then, that Ms. Brand, Ms. Philip and those who espouse their views see in me a right-wing racist dedicated to the preservation of imperialist colonialism. It may come as a surprise, though, that I have also been called a communist for an article I wrote on Spanish fascism, a social-democrat for writing about social evils, a feminist for exploring the situation of women. There is, in fact, hardly a label that has not been tossed at me, each ill-fitting, each contradicted by something else I've written. It is the risk run by a writer whose fiction arises from political concerns, more specifically from the effect of politics on the everyday lives of ordinary people. I have no ideology to sell and am resigned to the fact that there will never be any shortage of those who will try to define me and my work in political terms rarely favourable.

The accusations levelled against me and a variety of other artists across the country have in the end little to do with racism or sexism or any other "ism." These are simply convenient hooks that have much more to do with the revealed hollowness of armchair revolutionary ideology. Challenged where it hurts most, those who see themselves in my characters hit back like children, with a stunning if typical simple-mindedness. All artistic expression—whether a book, a painting or a museum exhibition—demands a certain subtlety of mind, a certain emotional nakedness, if it is to be understood. Ideologues, pushed by often legitimate grievances into a mind-numbing self-righteousness, have neither. Living by received ideas, they bend and simplify the complexities of life to suit their own ideological preoccupations. They seek to cow everyone else into accepting their visions and their timetables.

Those who seek to subordinate art, its functions and its freedoms to sexual, racial or religious politics seek nothing less than to impose their own ideological visions on the imaginative expressions of others. They claim rights for themselves that they would deny to those who do not share their view of the world.

In this society, the charge of racism is a particularly virulent one. There are few who do not recognize racism as an evil, making it a charge easily levelled by those who interpret the world through the colour of their skin, by those who are "racialized." Declaring themselves anti-racists, they ironically share a racial vision of life with the architects and defenders of apartheid. I would suggest that to define yourself by your colour is to be racist, just as to define yourself by your gender is sexist; it is to reduce the complexity of human beings to formulae. I would further suggest that imposed political ideology distorts reality, and that sharpened racial ideology distorts the soul.

When applied to the arts, imposed ideology has deadly consequences. In the United States, right-wing sensibilities essentially turned controversial photographer Robert Mapplethorpe into a pornographer, while in Toronto similar sensibilities led to the seizure by police of controversial paintings and drawings by a young painter named Eli Langer in December 1993.

Ideological concerns can also be imposed from within, though, and with consequences no less deadly. The finest example I know of this is the novel *Mother*, by the brilliant Soviet writer Maxim Gorky. Gorky produced many vivid and penetrating works througout his illustrious career, but none of his writing entranced the first leader of the Soviet state so much as *Mother*. Lenin declared it to be Gorky's best novel, while Gorky himself recognized it as by far his worst. The problem, as Gorky well understood, was that the book was too willed, the characters too manipulated, his concerns consciously constructed with political ends in mind. He had subordinated literature to politics and had produced a politically pleasing work that was also a static and artificial novel.

Ideological considerations can also infect reviews. Timothy Mo is a young and talented British novelist whose first three novels (*Sour Sweet, The Monkey King, An Insular Possession*) have been short-listed for the prestigious Booker prize in the U.K., as was his latest novel, a brilliant exploration of the nature of courage and commitment entitled *The Redundancy of Courage*. It is the story of a young Chinese man named Adolph Ng who is caught up in a situation closely resembling the Indonesian occupation of East Timor. A lukewarm review of the novel in *The Globe and Mail* questioned the authenticity of Mo's depiction of Adolph Ng, in part on the grounds that, while Ng is pure Chinese, Timothy Mo—whose mother is English—is only half so. The reviewer's other objection was that "the narrator is too unlike [the author] in experience"—a hesitation presumably never experienced by Shakespeare when he was writing *Hamlet* or by Tolstoy when he was writing *Anna Karenina*. The power of the imagination, then, is—if not discounted—at least viewed with suspicion. All of which prompts the question: must declarations of life experience and affidavits of racial and ethnic composition now be submitted with novel manuscripts (not to mention with job or conference applications)? It would represent the ultimate ordering of the multicultural society.

Ideological considerations have also led to calls for publishers to publish an imposed quota of "minority" writers,[24] regardless of the quality of the work. Notions of quality, the argument goes, are nothing but the artificial inventions of white males who, seeking to prolong their control of society, use tools—such as "Eurocentric" ideas of excellence—to keep ethnics and females on the edges of the mainstream. It needs to be said that such ideas are the products of the talentless, who, grown sanctimonious, seek a kind of artistic welfare to support their fantasies.

The academic world, too, has been severely affected. An idea making the rounds in some university literature departments suggests that, since male professors are by their very nature incapable of fully grasping the female point of view, they should not be allowed to teach novels by women writers. (A similar argument could be made that, say, Northrop Frye would have been incapable of teaching a novel by the African Nobel prize winner Wole Soyinka.) It occurs to few, one professor commented, that if men should not teach Atwood or Akhmatova, then, on the same grounds, female professors should not teach Shakespeare or Chaucer. The notion is one that would diminish the very idea of a university, reducing our perspectives on great, or even not so great, works of literature through attitudes reminiscent of a spiteful child refusing to let others play with his baseball simply because, in his opinion, they play less well.

Doreen Kimura, a neuro-psychologist at Simon Fraser University, a senior professor with over twenty-five years of experience, delivered the convocation speech at the University of Western Ontario on June 3, 1993. What she had to say was as revealing as it was distressing.

Professor Kimura spoke in defence of the right to academic freedom—a freedom which, in its very essence, must entail the right to disturb and even to offend. As a biological scientist, she pointed out, she deals in provocative ideas. Her research on brain and behaviour, for example, which entails the notion that all behaviour is a function of the nervous system and not of a soul, might challenge the basic beliefs of certain religious fundamentalists. Nor might some feminists take kindly to the idea that sex is a contributing factor in the way human brains are organized, in the way "individuals differ from each other in their special intellectual talents." The "offending of students in an intellectual sense," she insisted, is very much the role of a university: it is only through having their basic beliefs and assumptions challenged that students learn and grow.

It is with this background that Professor Kimura went on to detail the atmosphere created by some students who are offended by being offended:

> I unfortunately know of colleagues both within and outside my own university who have had their courses invaded by members of special-interest tribunals, merely because they were socially controversial. A professor at York University has had observers stationed in his class on a day when he discussed the evolution of behavioral differences between men and women. A watchdog committee has been set up at the University of Toronto to ensure that no references made in textbooks could be construed as unfavourable to any minority, no matter how factual or well-established such references are.
>
> These are not isolated events, unfortunately, but have become commonplace now, at least in eastern universities. The graduands of today will be too young to recall the reports of invasion of university classes by fascist partisans

> in Europe in the thirties, but some of the parents here today may recall such tactics. In fact, totalitarian regimes typically begin with the suppression of free speech. Can we honestly claim there is any fundamental difference between the Communist and fascist control of academia of the past and the suppression of ideas which is spreading throughout our campuses today?[25]

What takes root in the university setting has a way of spreading out into the larger society. The intimidation Professor Kimura details is today a fact of life for many in the academic and artistic communities.

At Trent University in Peterborough, Ontario, a group of professors have signed a petition asking for the right to be offensive, an action they took in light of a policy order issued in October 1993 by the Ontario Department of Education and Training. Aimed at respecting everyone's dignity, the order "prohibits discrimination for any of the usual reasons (race, creed, sex, sexual orientation, disability, age) plus a few that aren't so usual (dialect, accent, 'the receipt of public assistance, record of provincial offences or pardoned federal offences')."[26] None of these grounds is unsettling, but the order then tosses out a sentence of astonishing possibility: "A complainant does not have to be a direct target to be adversely affected by a negative environment."

A negative environment: Imagine, as Robert Fulford postulates,[27] the possibility for accusations of racism by a native student in a class run by a professor opposed to native sovereignty; the possibility of severe discomfort for male students in a class run by a feminist professor; the "negative environments" in classes where Jews are asked to study *The Merchant of Venice*, blacks required to read *Othello* and women to read *Ulysses*. Negative environments—environments of discomfort and distress—are part of the normal functioning of a university: only government bureaucrats and unformed minds fail to understand that, as Mr. Fulford puts it, being offended is part of learning how to think.

Fear of giving offence has even touched the judiciary, as Supreme Court Justice John Sopinka pointed out in a speech to Concordia University's political science students' association: "Judges in the past have, on occasion, been insensitive to the legitimate concerns of minority or disadvantaged groups. However, there is cause for legitimate concern that overzealous dissection of every word that drops from the bench, with a view to finding some political incorrectness which may be the basis for a complaint to the Judicial Council, may result in decisions that are politically correct but not legally and factually correct. A judge who is looking over his or her shoulder may decide a case in a way that will avoid the Judicial Council rather than accord with the material presented."[28]

It is at Concordia University, too, that concerns over freedom of speech have led to the establishment of the Society for Intellectual Freedom, a club, one of the student organizers said, for people to speak without having to look over their shoulders.

It is no secret that ideology of all kinds, stringently applied, has a way of eventually eating its own children. Reaganist greed, for instance, consumed platefuls of its own adherents.

While in Vancouver on a book-promotion tour some years ago, I met a young woman with an interesting story to tell. It is important to know that she considered herself a dyed-in-the-wool feminist. She told me about an article she had written about her favourite singer, a black American woman of great talent and renown. She submitted the piece to a feminist magazine that had published her work in the past. After some time, the editors informed her that, while they very much liked the article, they would not publish it. She had, they explained, quoted too many male critics. Her explanation—that most music critics are male—and her suggestion that publishing female writers might help change that situation made no impression. Their basic objection to the article was that while the singer was black, the writer was white—an intolerable situation in their view. The article, on purely racial grounds, could never be good enough.

Such limitations on subject matter lead to chilling logical conclusions. For does this not mean that young women must not write about old women, gay men about straight men, Protestants about Catholics? Does this not mean that physically handicapped writers must write only about the physically handicapped and native writers only about natives—indeed, a Cree writer only about Crees, a Mohawk writer only about Mohawks? In the end, then, does this view not say that fiction, and even nonfiction, must give way to autobiography? (On a lighter note, and from a different field, this would deny us the pleasure of what may be the best example of cultural appropriation ever seen: the Jamaican Olympic bobsled team.)

"Find your own river," Nigerian writer Chinua Achebe once said of Conrad's *Heart of Darkness*. "Don't appropriate our geography for your psychic journeys."[29] It is a curious notion, this idea of appropriation. After all, the river and all that it represents are still there, even after Kurtz has journeyed its length. Nothing prevents Achebe, a writer of distinction and international success, from sending one of his own characters on a journey into its brilliance and its darknesses—or along the brilliance and darknesses of the Thames, the Mississippi or the St. Lawrence. What precisely have Achebe and other African writers lost from Conrad's psychic exploration up a tropical river? The world has gained a masterpiece, and I for one am glad that Conrad accompanied Kurtz on that journey. To restrict Kurtz to the Thames is to demand an impoverishment of imagination.

It must be pointed out that, in her *Brick* article, Ms. Brand explicitly disassociates herself from any attempts at censorship. She kindly states that "Neil Bissoondath may write in any voice he pleases." However, in an interview with Dagmar Novak in 1990, Ms. Brand took quite a different stand on white writers tackling native themes: "I think I can say categorically that whites cannot write about native life." *Should not?* she is asked. "Should not. Yes, should not and cannot,"[30] she replies. It is not an external censorship she calls for, then, but an internal censorship—which is even more deadening to the imaginative life.

A free society depends on a multiplicity of voices and visions, on the interplay of conflicting views. We would only diminish ourselves by diminishing that variety. The terms of this debate are altering perceptions of art, of both its nature and its role, and that is healthy. But I fear too that the undignified tone of the debate—the name-calling, the creation of martyrs—is demeaning the arts in grim and objectionable ways. The "debate" in the Writers' Union over accusations of racism against June Callwood led (after several vicious anti-Callwood letters, some anonymous, some not) to ten of Canada's most elegant writers issuing a letter suggesting that "everyone should *shut the fuck up* for a period of remorseful consideration."[31] The "debate" over the "Writing Thru Race" conference ended inconclusively after "a shouting match broke out...with about 150 union members squaring off."[32] All perspectives on every issue of contention should be welcome—as citizens of a free society, we will all be the richer for it—but no one has the right to try to suppress the voice of anyone else, no matter how objectionable that voice may be.

Any attempt to padlock the mind is a question of fundamental liberty. Any limitation of subject matter or point of view, whether imposed from without or within, represents for us all a severe restriction on the free play of the imagination. As Salman Rushdie has pointed out, as far as writers are concerned, you have to feel that you write in absolute freedom—and freedom of expression means nothing if it does not include the freedom to offend.

On this issue, the Writers' Union of Canada took a more definite stand. In a resolution passed in June 1992, the Union "resolutely" affirmed "the freedom of imagination and the freedom of expression of all writers everywhere." Quickly following this statement, however, were six clauses beginning with either "But whereas" or "And whereas"—their own little versions of notwithstanding clauses. The endorsement of imaginative freedom is then qualified in one way or another in recognition that "cultural misappropriation exists as a form of oppression." It ends with the declaration that the Union "recognizes and affirms the responsibility and accountability that attend the freedom of imagination and the freedom of expression." This has been described by some as a call for the exercise of sensitivity, a praiseworthy goal to be sure. But, in the realm of cultural appropriation, who is to decide what is sensitive, what responsible? And are these qualities not judged on essentially political, non-literary criteria? And how much sensitivity, what definition of responsibility, will be acceptable to political activists for whom the very notion of writing about a culture not one's own is anathema?

While prettied up, this stand by the Writers' Union of Canada is less a resolution than an irresolution.

As far as writers are concerned, it is clear that those who advocate the padlocking of the imagination, or who demand that the imaginations of others proceed in prescribed ways, are profoundly ignorant of the writing process.

In an interview, Timothy Findley once said, "In the gay community they say, 'When are you going to write *the* gay novel?' But I don't define my life by my sexuality. I'm not a *gay* writer, I'm not a *male* writer, I'm just a writer."

Just a writer: those three words lie at the heart of it.

In a way, to be a writer of fiction is the simplest of jobs. It is to be a story-teller, nothing more, nothing less. But to tell a good story, and to tell it well, is a demanding, at times mysterious, process. To be *just a writer* is to be prey, to a great extent, to the demands and urges of the writing process itself.

A description of my writing process—and it is a little different for each writer—must begin with what I do *not* do.

I do not sit at my computer and think: I will write a story today about a black woman or a Jewish man and offend somebody—for to do so would be to engage in journalism. I do not decide that I will write a story to score points about racism or socialism or capitalism—for to do so would be to engage in propaganda. I avoid at all costs playing the role of puppeteer, manipulating my characters, telling them what to think or how to act, insisting on their being politically or socially correct. For to do any of the above would be to kill all possibility of spinning credible fiction.

The most hackneyed advice to young writers is: Write about what you know. Describe, in other words, what you have experienced. It is good advice—so long as one remembers that there are many ways of experiencing an event. Writing about what you know does not mean writing only about what you have *lived*. It includes all that you have come to understand or appreciate through conversation, observation, reading, dreaming, films—the many tributaries to the human imagination. The brain is a remarkable instrument; it is not one-dimensional and almost always knows things we are not conscious of. It constantly processes that information, adding, retrieving, shifting, connecting. It is in this way that originality occurs.

Precisely how my fiction comes about, then, is not easily explained. It is a process of the mind, and when I am asked, as I frequently am, where I get my ideas for stories, I can offer no coherent answer. The truth is that I do not really know. What happens is this: I do not find the stories, they find me.

Characters will emerge unbidden, often arising from stories or events that have etched themselves in my subconscious, their voices sometimes speaking at the most inconvenient of moments (such as when I'm in the shower or doing the dishes). When a voice is compelling, when it begins to relate its tale, I do my best, with the language I have at my disposal, to capture on paper what it says or shows to me. I follow the voice into its world, grateful for its generosity, constrained by its reticence. And it is in the writing that I discover who the character is, and what story he or she has to tell. It is in the writing, word by word, sentence by sentence, that I discover my characters' appearances and lives, their joys and their pains. Nothing is planned, nothing is decided ahead of time. Plot and structure will take care of themselves, shaped by the revelations of the voices in my head—voices that belong to strangers I slowly get to know, word by word, sentence by sentence. It is rare, when I begin working on a story, that I know what the outcome will be—and even when I do know, I never have any idea of how we will get there. Frequently, in the writing, my own story will surprise me. This is the thrill of writing fiction: being led into a world, into lives, never anticipated.

If the characters live, they will at times do and say things I dislike or with which I disagree, but this, far from detracting from their validity, lends them a greater integrity. In "Immoral Fiction," Marlene Philip sees misogyny in my depiction of a female character. The character is not physically attractive; she is described as "slack faced," her complexion is pasty, her breasts are pendulous. I could, I suppose, have intervened to make her a more attractive woman. But she was not; the world is full of men and women who are not attractive. Literary characters are not the writer's playthings; they are not lumps of clay to be moulded into idealized portraits. If they are true, they should be fully developed individuals with minds and lives of their own, existing within the imaginative world of the writer.

Literary characters must be true only to themselves and their circumstances. They owe allegiance to neither the writer nor the social group to which they belong. They are, if they truly live, individuals with their own psychology and their own biography, no more and no less representative or symbolic of a group than any live, breathing human being. The portrait to which Ms. Philip took such a dislike is not meant as a representative of Canadian Womanhood; the character represents only herself.

To oblige characters to adopt a preordained stance is to kill those characters. It is to take away their individuality, to remove their freedom of choice. When ideological concerns are allowed precedence over artistic ones, the art—the short story, the novel, the film—emerges dull and lifeless, the artistic achievement sacrificed to the political document, the role of fiction in particular subverted.

Just as Timothy Findley does not define his writing by his gender or his sexuality, so I do not define my writing by my gender or my colour. A writer's concerns go far beyond these boxes, extending to a wider humanity. The Nobel-prize-winning novelist Nadine Gordimer, a white female guilty of writing from perspectives neither white nor female, once explained it succinctly: "When it comes to their essential faculty as writers," Ms. Gordimer once wrote, "all writers are androgynous beings." It is for this reason that the notion of cultural or voice appropriation is devoid of artistic legitimacy.

But there is another reason for this lack of legitimacy, and it has to do with the role of fiction as I perceive it.

My primary goal as a writer, as I have already stated, is to tell a good story, to entertain. But it is in part, too, the challenge of capturing as precisely as language will allow a tiny slice of the human experience and sharing that feeling, that perception, with others. I also aim in my writing to question harsh realities and challenge accepted verities, to offer new angles on old truths.

But the urge to write goes beyond this, for one also hopes for a grander effect. And what could be grander than shedding light, to the best of one's ability, on the unknown? This is why I am attracted in my fiction to characters pointedly different from myself. Writing is for me neither autobiography nor therapy. It is, first and foremost, an act of discovery. I seek, through literary exploration, to understand lives very different from my own, pursuing what I would call the demystification of the Other.

It is only through true understanding of others that we can ever hope to make real progress against racism, sexism and all the other evils that afflict us. Only by replacing ignorance with knowledge—not the rhetoric of politics, not the simplicities of multicultural stereotypes, but the intimate details of single lives—can we hope to move beyond them. It is precisely because I have not lived the life that I seek to explore and, I hope, understand it—and, with luck, to help others understand it too. This is why I do not write about communities, racial or ethnic. This is the reason I write about individuals. In my fiction, humanity is not my concern. Humans are.

In June 1990, the playwright Joanna Glass wrote in *The Globe and Mail* about the Second International Women Playwrights Conference in Toronto. She wrote with undisguised pain and undiluted anger of encountering a preponderance of politics. She told with embarrassment of the Soviet playwright who saw her translator evicted for being male, of two foreign playwrights who were openly ridiculed after admitting their heterosexuality. She described various "bevies" holding up signs of identification: "Women of Colour" said one; "Women of Pallor" said another. Lamenting the lack of serious playwrights and the absence of all discussion of craft, Ms. Glass wondered plaintively why she had to search so hard to find the Women of Talent. As it was with the Women Playwrights Conference, so it is in the "debates" on voice appropriation and "Writing Thru Race." The Women of Talent, one suspects, were at their desks, working at their craft. "I believe it is important to point out," Ms. Glass wrote, "that the rabble-rousers are not unlike the wife-beaters of the gender they so despise. They are bullies. Their behaviour should not be condoned by anyone, of any political or sexual persuasion.

They severely hinder our cause."

Rabble-rousers rouse the rabble in order to get attention. It is advisable always to decipher what they say, to judge the legitimacy not only of their complaints but of their proposals, to separate the sensible from the senseless, the significant from the insignificant, the genuine from the fake. The task is to determine who, or what, in other words, are deserving of continuing attention.

In *Brick*, Dionne Brand took exception to my story "The Cage" and its portrait of a young Japanese woman seeking freedom in a new land. It only "revalidates the myth of the 'Oriental woman' in Eurocentric discourse," she writes. It is criticism, though, that must be weighed against the more positive reaction of a variety of other women, most memorably a young Malaysian woman who, after reading the story, commented to a mutual friend that, although we had never met, she felt I had understood something vital about her own life.

Marlene Philip takes my novel *A Casual Brutality* to task for its political incorrectness—and this too is criticism that must be weighed against the words of a young Ethiopian man who sought me out to say that the novel, set in Toronto and the Caribbean, held haunting resonances for him.

And political objections lose all meaning before the embarrassing gratitude of the young Romanian refugee who, after a school reading of a story about a Latin-American refugee claimant, thanked me for explaining to her classmates more clearly than she could what it was like to live the life of a refugee.

If I indulge in some of the positive comments my work has received, it is only to contrast the reactions of non-political readers against the complaints of politically motivated ones. It is an attempt to show where the true importance of artistic expression lies.

I trust no one who claims to speak in the name of the People. The People have their own voice. Rabble-rousers represent no constituency save their own ideological obsessions. Their message is one of negation and division, seeking to erect "multicultural," apartheid-like walls around the ghettos of ethnic and cultural communities. They are loud—but this does not mean they are right.

Politics in painting. Politics in writing. Politics in the theatre. It is curious that artists, who rarely pay heed to the homilies of politicians, should pay such heed to the homilies of those who are politicians in all but name. The psychology and politics of multiculturalism have made divisiveness in the name of racial and ethnic rights socially acceptable. They have given legitimacy here to what was once deplored in racially segregated South Africa. Led by a policy apparently benign, betrayed by our own sensitivities, we have come a full and curious circle.

A kind of courage is required now, the courage to recognize foolishness and to say no to it: the courage of common sense and true sensitivity displayed by the publisher of "The Hockey Sweater" who, in refusing the request to delete the references to God from the story, pointed out that "one of the purposes of education is to foster tolerance of the varying backgrounds and beliefs of others sharing this planet."

As a writer, I will continue to practise my craft. I will continue, as will many others, to tell the stories of the men and women who present themselves to my imagination, regardless of race, regardless of gender. I will continue to pursue, to the best of my ability, the demystification of the Other.

Nine

Endings

Nobody knows what you integrate to any more. Before the First World War, you had the sense that here you had an Anglo-Saxon Protestant matrix and an imperial British culture—and everybody knew what hymn we were all singing. Now the question is, who's defining the context of integration at all, and what kind of Canada are you integrating yourself to?

Michael Ignatieff in conversation
December 1, 1993

Ethnicity

Divisiveness is a dangerous playmate, and few playgrounds offer greater scope for divisiveness than that of ethnicity. The walls are high, ready-made, as solid as obsession. Guard towers can be built, redoubts that allow defence and a distant view into the land of the other. Like all walls, they can be either accepted as integral to life or breached—dismantled brick by brick—as restrictive to it. How to view those walls, how or even if to deal with them, is a decision each individual must make.

For society at large, though, ethnicity and its walls must be barriers to nothing. No opportunity must be denied, no recognition withheld, no advancement refused. Neither, however, must ethnicity be claimed as grounds for opportunity, recognition or advancement. Tempting though it may be, a multicultural society can ill afford the use of past discrimination as justification for future recrimination. It is essential, in such a society, that discrimination be permissible only on the basis of knowledge and ability. To do otherwise—to discriminate, for instance, against white males as a class because of transgressions by other white males in the past—is to employ the simplistic eye-for-an-eye, tooth-for-a-tooth philosophy implicit in arguments supportive of capital punishment. There is an element of class vengeance to it, an element of self-righteousness, that offers victims or their descendants the opportunity to strike back. It is like arguing that the victims of torture must be allowed to torture their torturers. Redress is important, but the nature of that redress is even more so, for it sets the tone for the future. Yesterday cannot be changed, but tomorrow is yet to be shaped, and ways must be found to avoid creating resentments today that might lead to upheavals tomorrow. As Nelson Mandela has made clear, a peaceful and prosperous future for a multi-racial South Africa cannot be secured through punitive action for the wrongs of the past; it can be attained only through the full recognition of human dignity implicit in the acceptance of equality.

Economic and social imbalance cannot be redressed overnight. Only revolution can effect so radical a change, and if there is a lesson to be learned from the history of the twentieth century it is that revolutionary change is illusory: it merely changes oppressors and the nature of oppression. True and lasting change, then, cannot be imposed; it must come slowly, growing with experience, from within.

The comment was once made that racism is as Canadian as maple syrup. History provides us with ample proof of that. But perspective requires the notation that racism is also as American as apple pie, as French as croissants, as Indian as curry, as Jamaican as Akee, as Russian as vodka... It's an item on every nation's menu. Racism, an aspect of human virulence, is exclusive to no race, no country, no culture, no civilization. This is not to excuse it. Murder and rape, too, are international, multicultural, innate to the darker side of the human experience. But an orderly and civil society requires that the inevitable rage evoked not blind us to the larger context.

The word "racism" is a discomforting one: it is so easily vulnerable to manipulation. We can, if we so wish, apply it to any incident involving people of different colour: had June Callwood directed her infamous two words at a white woman, it would have been virtually impossible to slander her with the charge of racism. Therein lies the danger. During the heat of altercation, we seize, as terms of abuse, on whatever is most obvious about the other person—or what we may perceive as being a point of emotional (or, as in Ms. Callwood's case, political) vulnerability. A woman, because of her sex, can easily become an intimate part of her anatomy colloquially described (as, indeed, can men). A large person might be dubbed a stupid ox, a small person a shrimp or a pip-squeak. And so a black person might be dubbed a "nigger," a white a "honky," an Asian a "paki," a Chinese a "chink," an Italian a "wop," a Jew a "kike," a French-Canadian a "frog."

There is nothing pleasant about these terms: they are demeaning; they constitute an assault on every decent sensibility. Even so, I once met someone who, with a stunning naïvety, used them as simple descriptives and not as terms of abuse. She was horrified to learn the truth. While this may have been an extreme case, the point is that the use of such patently abusive words might not always indicate racial or cultural distaste. It may indicate ignorance, stupidity, insensitivity—but we can be thankful that pure racial hatred, of the Nazi or Ku Klux Klan type, remains, in this society, a rare commodity. There is, thanks to our history of civility, something unCanadian about it. For most people, I would suspect, the blatant racists among us are a source of embarrassment.

Ignorance, not the wilful kind but that which comes from lack of experience and uninformed assumption, is often indicated by the defensive phrase, "I'm not racist but..." I think of a mover, a friendly man, who once said to me, "I'm not racist, but the Chinese are the worst drivers on the road." He was convinced that this was so because the shape of their eyes, as far as he could surmise, denied them peripheral vision.

There is something similar in the vision of the man who rejected apartment buildings with East Indian tenants because of their rumoured love for gift-wrapped cockroaches—as there is in the pitifully angry voices of Canadian Legion members as they reject the imposition on them of a rule that would lessen their control of the last space within their influence. Few of these people would think of themselves as racist, and the charge would undoubtedly be wounding to most, if not all of them, and yet their comments, often so innocently delivered, would open them up to the accusation.

True racism is based, more often than not, on wilful ignorance and an acceptance of and comfort with stereotype. We like to think, in this country, that our multicultural mosaic will help nudge us into a greater openness. But multiculturalism as we know it indulges in stereotype, depends on it for a dash of colour and the flash of dance—and that in itself is not a bad thing. But such an approach fails to address the most basic questions people have about each other: Do those men doing the Dragon Dance really all belong to secret criminal societies? Do those women dressed in saris really coddle cockroaches for luck? Do those people in dreadlocks all smoke marijuana and live on welfare in between criminal acts? Such questions do not seem to be the concern of multiculturalism in Canada. Far easier is indulgence in the superficial and the exhibitionistic.

Community response to racism, while important, must also be measured, responsible. We must beware the self-appointed activists who seem to pop up in the media at every given opportunity, spouting the rhetoric of retribution, mining distress for personal, political and professional gain. We must beware those who depend on conflict for their sense of self: the non-whites who need to feel themselves victims of racism, the whites who need to feel themselves purveyors of it. We must be certain that in addressing the problem we do not end up creating it. I do not know if the Miss Black Canada Beauty Pageant still exists, but it is my fervent hope that it does not. Not only are beauty contests in themselves offensive, a racially segregated one is even more so. What would public reaction be, I wonder, if every year television offered a broadcast of a Miss White Canada Beauty Pageant? There are community-service awards given exclusively to blacks: would we be comfortable with such awards given exclusively to whites? If we acccept a racially exclusive conference for non-white writers, should we not also accept one for white writers? Quebec offers the Association of Black Nurses, the Association of Black Artists, the Congress of Black Jurists. Replace Black with White and watch the dancing visions of apartheid. It is inescapable that racism for one is racism for the other.

It is vital, also, that we beware of abusing the word itself. Let us be certain that we apply it only when it is merited. Doing so not only avoids a harmful backlash but also ensures that we do not empty the word of meaning, that we do not constantly cry wolf by seeing racism as rampant and systemic, and so drain it of emotional potency. "Racism" remains a dirty word in Canada. It must be kept that way.

The Tolerant Society

In a radio interview, the novelist Robertson Davies once spoke of the difference between two words that are often—and erroneously—used interchangeably: acceptance and tolerance.

Acceptance, he pointed out, requires true understanding, recognition over time that the obvious difference—the accent, the skin colour, the crossed eyes, the large nose—are mere decoration on the person beneath. It is a meeting of peoples that delves under the surface to a knowledge of the full humanity of the other.

Tolerance, on the other hand, is far more fragile, for it requires not knowledge but wilful ignorance, a purposeful turning away from the accent, the skin colour, the crossed eyes, the large nose. It is a shrug of indifference that entails more than a hint of condescension.

The pose of tolerance is seductive, for it requires no effort; it is benign in that it allows others to get on with their lives free of interference—and also free of a helping hand. The problem, of course, is that tolerance—based as it is on ignorance—can, with changing circumstances, give way to a perception of threat. And such a perception is all that is required to cause a defensive reaction to kick in—or to lash out. Already in this country, we are seeing the emergence of reaction from those who feel themselves and their past, their beliefs and their contribution to the country, to be under assault. People who are "put up with" in the good times assume aspects of usurpers in the bad. Notions of purity—both cultural and racial—come to the forefront as the sense of self diminishes under the assault of unemployment, homelessness, a growing sense of helplessness.

This tolerance can very quickly metamorphose into virulent defensiveness, rejecting the different, alienating the new. Understanding, in contrast, requires effort, a far more difficult proposition, but may lead to acceptance and, for the newcomers, a sense of belonging. Multiculturalism, with its emphasis on the easy and the superficial, fosters the former while ignoring the latter.

Canada has long prided itself on being a tolerant society, but tolerance is clearly insufficient in the building of a cohesive society. A far greater goal to strive for would be an *accepting* society. Multiculturalism seems to offer at best provisional acceptance, and it is with some difficulty that one insists on being a full—and not just an associate—member of society. Just as the newcomer must decide how best to accommodate himself or herself to the society, so the society must in turn decide how it will accommodate itself to the newcomer. Multiculturalism has served neither interest; it has heightened our differences rather than diminished them; it has preached tolerance rather than encouraging acceptance; and it is leading us into a divisiveness so entrenched that we face a future of multiple solitudes with no central notion to bind us.

Quebec

It is its cosmopolitan nature that will ensure Montreal's future. I do not mean by that exotic restaurants, trendy boutiques or cafés; I mean a

> population that has come from all over the world, that accepts French as a natural fact, English as a convenient means of communication, and that will create a diversified culture grafted on a French-speaking tree.
>
> Jacques Godbout
> *The Globe and Mail*
> November 6, 1989

French Canada entered my consciousness in my second year at university through a course in Québécois literature. While the English-Canadian literature I had encountered seemed on the whole to be concerned with gentle days growing up on the Prairies, French-Canadian writing was striking in its intensity. Engaged, passionate, combative, informed by an anger both visceral and intellectual, it seemed designed to unsettle and incite rather than reassure. The honest brutality of the opening scene of Roch Carrier's *La Guerre, Yes Sir!*, in which Joseph axes off his own hand in order to avoid conscription into a war he sees as not his own, marked itself forever in my imagination, and the starkness of the scene tempered my surprise at the election, in 1976, of René Lévesque and the Parti Québécois.

So it *was* a surprise, during the year I spent in Quebec City (1985-86), to discover that far from being alienated by my speaking English, people were attracted to it. I learned that the language laws that incited so much anger in the rest of the country were intended as a social measure, not a personal one. Service in stores and restaurants and provincial government offices was offered in French and in English—which was at times irritating to someone who wished to practise his French. But more than this, the people of Quebec City were refreshingly friendly, candid in their curiosity. They were not unnerved by difference.

At dinner in a restaurant one evening with an English-speaking companion, a man at the next table interrupted our conversation to say how pleasing it was to hear English again. He was francophone, had moved from Montreal to Quebec City, and found that he missed the sounds of the language. It was, in its implications, a complex statement, for it spoke in subtle ways of the unacknowledged: of a true meeting of peoples; of shared history, shared visions, shared attitudes. It said that, because of overlapping influences and despite the differences between languages, provinces and regions, we have acquired an uneasy similarity. Though sometimes blinded by the immediacy of political concerns, we are as a people fundamentally blended: our interest in each other cannot easily be extinguished. The right arm may not resemble the left arm, but they belong together on the same body, serving its interests and their own. Each would be poorer without the other.

In Quebec City, one was simply included, accepted, seduced into feeling at home. The Plains of Abraham, historically poignant, assuredly federal, a gathering place for quiet pleasures, remains one of my favourite places in the country. Its open spaces and panoramic views of the St. Lawrence, its reminders of the past that has shaped us in such fundamental ways, speak on many levels, not all of them definable, to one's sense of belonging.

But Quebec City is one thing, Montreal quite another. More populous, more ethnically diverse, living directly with the challenge of other languages, its tensions—not only linguistic but social and economic, like those of any big city—are at times palpable. The city appears to have accommodated itself less successfully than Toronto or

Vancouver to its growing ethnic diversity, almost as if unwilling to accept the changes that would necessarily require it to surrender elements of its personality. While Vancouver and Toronto have proved able to reshape themselves, while they have eased into a remaking of the public face, Montreal, for so long the centre of Quebec's struggle to preserve its French character, holds greedily to its sense of self, to the *joie de vivre* that sometimes feels forced, manufactured. Probably because of the anxieties with which they live, Montrealers tend to be less open, more defensive, more self-protective than the people of Quebec City. They take themselves and their reputation very seriously—rather, it must be said, like Torontonians.

The point, simply put, is this: just as English Canada is no monolith of views, interests and attitudes, so Quebec is no monolith of views, interests and attitudes. And like English Canada and Quebec, no ethnic group, or "cultural community" as they are referred to in Quebec, is a monolith of views, interests and attitudes. To pretend otherwise is to indulge in the simplification of stereotype.

In Canada, the old colonial mentality—and I use the term descriptively—has been relegated, kicking and blustering, to the margins, but the attitude of dependence—the comforts of being a follower beholden to forces and traditions larger and older than our own—retains a certain appeal. In twenty-five years, we have moved from Pierre Trudeau, the free-thinker who wanted to sell his countrymen a vision, to Brian Mulroney, the free-trader who simply wanted to sell his countrymen; from an idea of ourselves as a fresh and exciting country that could set its own pace to another idea of ourselves that is simply a retreat to the comforts of yesteryear; from Pierre Trudeau pirouetting behind the Queen to Brian Mulroney catering to the continentalism of Ronald Reagan and George Bush; from deference to one set of betters, to a flirtation with independence, to deference to another set of betters.

It is a picture of social and political drift, of a desire to control our own destiny and a fear of doing so. There is something distasteful, we seem to think, in attempting to be all we can be. We end up, then, like a ship buffeted by winds that gust and probe their way through our disordered staterooms, the passengers lost and wandering, directionless, jealously seizing whatever they can grab while, on the bridge, would-be captains argue endlessly about the direction of Paradise.

One stateroom, though, has managed to batten down and order itself. Some of its passengers go so far as to eye a lifeboat as a means of salvation from the drifting ship.

Here, then, lies one of the essential differences between English-speaking Canada and the province of Quebec.

Beginning in the sixties and accelerating through the seventies, Canada was hurtling through social change. In English-speaking Canada, the old colonial centre was being swept away by waves of "non-traditional" immigrants, the old centre relegated to the margins, the new Canada redefining itself into a "cultural mosaic." At the same time, change of quite a different order was taking place in Quebec. The old church-ridden, agricultural society was remaking itself, modernizing itself, throwing off restraints both internal and external. While English Canada soon found itself adrift, with no sense of its centre, Quebec redefined its own centre, strengthened it, sought to make it unassailable. A host of economic measures ensured an economic future for a people long denied widespread prosperity, and a series of laws designed to protect the language and culture were put into place.

Simply put, then, while English Canada saw its defining Britishness dismantled, Quebec saw its defining Frenchness strengthened.

For a newcomer, the difference was striking.

In English Canada, the prevailing attitude seemed to be "Come as you are—Do as you please." The society had few expectations beyond adherence to the basic rule of law.

Quebec, however, was more demanding. The prevailing attitude was "Come as you are, but be prepared to engage with a French-speaking society." This meant that advancement would depend on your ability to work in French; it meant that your children would attend French schools; it meant that if you opened a convenience store, your signs must advertise LAIT not MILK, PAIN not BREAD, BIÈRE not BEER. The rules of the game may have been distasteful to some, they may have seemed oppressive to others, but they were clear. And when you stopped to think about it, you realized that Quebec had simply made *de jure* what was *de facto* elsewhere in the country: if a Spanish-speaker arrived in Toronto, he would necessarily have to live much of his life—to engage with the society—in English. Quebec was simply saying that, *chez nous*, the same thing must be done in French.

Le Devoir publisher Lise Bissonnette once wrote, "In the eyes of English Canadians, who like to believe that they practise the canons of multiculturalism, Québécois culture is just one stem in the great and colourful cultural bouquet which blossoms from coast to coast."[1] If multiculturalism was meant, in part, to cast Quebecers as just another ethnic group, to reduce the distinctiveness of the province's history and place in Confederation to parity with the other provinces, then it has worked to a large extent—outside Quebec at least. Evidence of this is found in the resistance to affording the province special constitutional status; the insistence that it is simply one of ten equal provinces, with the same powers, same rights, same obligations. But this is a simple-minded view of equality. It is obvious to anyone with a nodding acquaintance of Quebec that it is different. It has obligations—to its language, to its culture, to its view of life—that the other provinces do not. And if you have special obligations, then you need special powers to fulfil those obligations. But if Quebecers are just another ethnic group, their needs can be, politically speaking, safely ignored.

The problem, of course, is that Quebecers themselves have never bought into the Canadian idea of multiculturalism. Its dangers were self-evident. "Carried over into Quebec," Ms. Bissonnette has written, "this multiculturalism would be suicidal, since it tends to make francophones a minority like the others."

In addition, reservations have been expressed by Claude Corbo, rector of l'Université du Québec à Montréal and himself the grandson of Italian immigrants. Declaring multiculturalism to be a dead-end for immigrants, Mr. Corbo pointed out that the policy has kept many "from integrating naturally into the fabric of Canadian and Quebec society."[2] He called for its abolition, adding that "We tell people to preserve their original patrimony, to conserve their values, even if these values are incompatible with those of our society."

Quebec is no haven for immigrants. It too has its share of racists, and an undeniable strain of xenophobia runs through its nationalism. Parti Québécois leader Jacques Parizeau has mused in the past about an independent Quebec reducing the number of English-language radio and television stations in the province to reflect the percentage of anglophones—which is, philosophically at least, a gesture of tyranny. And it is M. Parizeau too who indulges in intimidation of financial institutions that question the benefits of separatism to the Quebec economy. These are not ideas that reassure.

Certain linguistic expressions, too, prove unsettling. "*Québécois pure laine*," an identification that hints of notions of racial purity, causes me to reflect that my "*laine*" will never be "*pure*" enough to allow me, in the eyes of some, to fully belong to the family: I will always be the Other. "*Le Québec aux Québécois*," the vociferous chant of the crowds marching in celebration of St.-Jean-Baptiste, evokes the question of who is a Quebecer—and the politically expedient answer first offered by René Lévesque and parroted by nationalist spokesmen ever since, that a Quebecer is anyone who lives in Quebec, is at best disingenuous, for it implies an absurd corollary: If a Quebecer is anyone who lives in Quebec, then a Quebecer who leaves the province ceases to be a Quebecer, unless, one imagines, the Quebecer happens to be "*pure laine*" or "*de vielle souche*." The answer, meant to disarm, is meaningless.

The notion of who is a Quebecer has an unhappy history. Even René Lévesque, that most cosmopolitan and trustworthy of separatists, a man who refused to reduce social and ethical complexities to political simplicities, was nevertheless prey to unsettling notions of purity. He once declared that Pierre Elliott Trudeau "has no particularly strong roots in the Quebec identity and culture. This is just a fact. He is half Scottish and anglophone through his mother, and French-Quebecan [sic] through his father."[3] Is it possible, then, for someone with no French roots to be a Quebecer? During the 1980 referendum campaign, Lévesque stung Trudeau by sneering at the Elliott in his name: "Mr. Lévesque said that Elliott is part of my name, and because Elliott is English that somehow explains why I'm on the No side, because I'm not a real Québécois.... And this is the contempt the Parti Québécois shows, to say that some people are real Québécois and some aren't, but the Yes supporters have pure blood in their veins.... Yes, my name is Elliott! Elliott is my mother's name. The Elliotts came here 200 years ago and settled in St. Gabriel de Brandon, and my name is Québécois!"[4]

Some see a shift away from such racial thinking, though. *La Presse* columnist Lysiane Gagnon, for example, noted that "Anything that smacks of 'ethnic purity' is definitely passé. Nowadays, the 'correct' way to be a sovereignist is to emphasize the territorial, rather than ethnic, dimension."[5] And yet it was not long ago that the notion of "real" Quebecers and traitorous Quebecers was raised. During the 1993 election campaign, Guy Boutin, Bloc Québécois candidate in Jean Charest's Sherbrooke riding, termed Mr. Charest a "traitor," adding that he was a Trudeau product ("C'est de la graine de Trudeau").[6] Much was also made at one point of the fact that Mr. Charest's name on his birth certificate is actually "John" and not "Jean."

And then, a few months later, Jean Campeau, co-chairman of the Bélanger-Campeau Commission and a star candidate for the Parti Québécois, said (in English): "If you're a real Quebecer you sympathize with the PQ."[7] Even though party spokesmen scrambled to downplay the remark, the implication was clear enough that André Boisclair, a party official with a reputation for defending the anglophone community within the PQ, publicly distanced himself from it. "A Quebecer is someone who lives in Quebec ..." he said. The idea, then, of the "provisional" Quebecer is not so very far away.

When Nancy Huston, a Calgary-born novelist who has lived for twenty years in France, was awarded the 1993 Governor General's Award for French fiction for her novel *Cantique des plaines*, protests were raised by several Quebec publishers who complained in *Le Devoir* that the choice did "a serious wrong to Canada's francophone authors." In *La Presse*, columnist Natalie Petrowski, a combative separatist not given to subtlety, joined the fray. Ignoring questions of literary merit—she admitted to not having read the book and, further, did not intend to—she pointed out that the prize has "almost always been given to Québécois" and that it was wrong to award it to "an exile, a wanderer without roots who not only does not write in her own language but no longer has any links with the land."[8] Without realizing it, Petrowski succeeded simply in making Huston's achievement seem even more brilliant—but that, of course, was not her intention, which was to belittle, to draw circles of purity around holy turf.

But still, there is undeniable evidence of a movement away from the narrow and the simplistic. In February 1994, former Liberal Jean Allaire announced the policy of his new party, le Parti Action démocratique du Québec, on immigration. While supportive of continued immigration, the party also proposed a plan of integration that would require immigrants to sign a contract committing them "to know and to appreciate francophone culture." The level of integration would be evaluated every six months over a period of five years, at the end of which, should the immigrant not measure up or wish to leave Quebec, he would have "to reimburse the state for the sum invested in integration." Describing the plan as "non-coercive," Mr. Allaire said, "If they don't want to accept the way things are here, why would they come?"[9]

The plan met with immediate and complete rejection. In *La Presse*, editorialist Agnès Gruda pronounced it the recipe for a police state. Lise Bissonnette in *Le Devoir* declared it reactionary, the product of "the Quebec tradition of muddle-headed and moralising protest." The *Montreal Gazette* called it "preposterous and grotesque." And even the Parti Québécois deemed it "stupid and contrary to the rights of individuals...manifestly illegal."

On a more positive note was an editorial in *Voir*, Montreal's unabashedly nationalist, cultural weekly, by editor Richard Martineau. Entitled "For a culture without a flag," the piece was categorical in its rejection of nationalist sentiment in judging cultural products:

> I may be Québécois and indépendantiste but Rita Mitsouko and U2 say more to me than Gilles Vigneault (who doesn't attract me in the least) and Marie Carmen. And Schindler's List stirs me more than Louis 19, even if it was made by a film-maker who never set foot in Chibougamau. When I write such things, it never fails—three or four people will accuse me of being traitorous and colonised.... Must we genuflect before any idiot just because he was born here, among us?... My ears don't give a damn about flags. They don't make any difference between a Quebec note and a Thai note. They react to notes that make them react, that's all there is to it.... The time when the label "made in Quebec" was enough to excite people is over. Now you've got to be good.... I prefer to listen to intelligent ideas in English than to nonsense in my own language. After all, I may be part of a people, but I am first and foremost an individual.[10]

These are the sentiments that comfort. These are the attitudes that embrace. Richard Martineau, one suspects, would have read and appreciated Nancy Huston's novel before commenting on the attribution of a prize.

And it is such attitudes—an insistence on going beyond one's own cultural borders to seek out a larger humanity—that bode well for the future.

Je me souviens, Quebec's official motto, is another way of saying "Never again!" It is also another way of saying, as some Canadian Legion members and RCMP veterans are saying, "Tradition!" But it is not possible to preserve the past. It is possible only to preserve a memory of it. And that memory is inevitably one of a variety of versions, each true and each false in its own way, personality and event filtered through the knowledge, ignorance, misconceptions, prejudices and selectiveness of the individual mind. For this reason, official versions of recollected event must be suspect; and for this reason, too, collective memory—the very idea of it, trimmed and pruned and interpreted with an eye to present-day prejudices—must also be suspect.

Only in this way could a certain number of Quebecers revere the memory of the anti-Semite nationalist Lionel Groulx sufficiently to name a major Metro station in his memory. To infer, though, that Quebecers as a group are anti-Semitic would be as accurate as to infer that erecting a statue of Mackenzie King, who regularly sought advice from his dog and his dead mother, indicates a widespread belief in spiritualism among Canadians. If the statistics are to be believed, anti-Semitism is no more prevalent in Quebec than elsewhere in the country, and rather less.

The point is that (as with the slave-owning Thomas Jefferson in the United States) aspects of a life can be rejected and others revered through the discrimination of memory. It is Groulx's nationalism that is honoured, not his racism. This disagreeable aspect of the man is ignored but not, it must be stressed, denied. Groulx has not been simplified into a nationalist hero; he—like former premier Maurice Duplessis, whose granite likeness gazes at the Grande Allée outside the Quebec legislature—has been claimed, warts and all, for the spotlight of history.

This accommodation of an individual to his historical importance takes time however.

On November 1, 1993, the sixth anniversary of René Lévesque's death, film-maker Claude Fournier, himself an ardent nationalist, published an unblushing biography of the former premier entitled *René Lévesque: Portrait d'un homme seul.* The book was not an exercise in hagiography. Instead, it attempted to capture both the light and the darkness, not only the driven man pursuing his political vision but also the compulsive man pursuing women and dry martinis. Neither did it flinch from exploring what Lysiane Gagnon describes as "the darkest episodes from his last year in power, when he often lost control of himself."[11] Quebec, unlike the rest of the continent, has historically chosen to ignore the personal peccadilloes of its politicians, so long as the private behaviour did not influence the public duties. It was not so with Lévesque during the second half of his second mandate, and Fournier's purpose was to construct a portrait of an essential loner undone by forces both internal and external, even if it meant shattering the iconic glow that has arisen around Lévesque's memory. But that memory, that glow, still have their political purposes for the separatist cause. To separatists, then, Fournier's book was, as Lysiane Gagnon put it, "little less than a sacrilege."

René Lévesque, unlike Groulx and Duplessis, has not yet been committed to history. But if the past is anything to go by, Quebec will one day be ready to accept him in his full, and not always attractive, humanity. It may even, one day, be prepared to accept Pierre Elliott Trudeau in his full, and not always attractive, complexity. For to accept the flawed humanity of Lévesque and the unsettling complexity of Trudeau will be to accept the humanity and complexity of the people of Quebec themselves. It will be a day that marks the definitive move away from concepts of "*Québécois pure laine*" and "*Québécois de souche*"—people who, in the words of Lise Bissonnette, "are still too often the champions of racial prejudice"[12]—and the acceptance of a truly open society.

There is a tension in Quebec between the old, racially minded nationalists and their modern, more cosmopolitan brethren. There are many questions, no easy answers—but the debate has been engaged, the hard questions are being asked, and there is the sense that the new is fast gaining ground on the old. To quote Lise Bissonnette once more: "The most urgent matter is that of the so-called 'multi-ethnic and French' Quebec. Quebec has failed to build a nest somewhere between angelic interculturalism and racism.... The model for integration remains vague and contradictory; it is not surprising that immigrants ignore it, or complain of a cold welcome.... Nonetheless there is no embarrassment in saying that Quebec wants to be French, that the francophone majority does not have to apologize for breathing its own air, and that different cultures can mingle with the French-speaking one."[13] In none of this intellectual ferment, then, is the essential notion of Quebec, its centre, its sense of self, questioned or surrendered. Far from it. As the 1978 Quebec white paper on cultural development put it:

> If French is to be Quebec's common language,

> as everyone seems to agree, then the cultural consequences must be accepted. Not, let it be repeated, because the French tradition must drive all others out of Quebec, but because the French culture, like the French language, should serve as a *focal point* for the various communities which will continue to make their presence felt and to express their own cultural values.[14]

In a brief to the Bélanager-Campeau Commission, the Quebec teachers' union, the CEQ, supported an open immigration policy while explicitly rejecting assimilation in favour of integration. Expressing complete disagreement with the imposition of any racial or cultural criteria, it emphasized that "the survival of the Quebec people and the protection of its common culture are not jeopardized by the presence in Quebec of persons of various origins, mother tongues or ethnic cultures. They could be jeopardized, however, by an ambiguity in the relationships between the ethnic groups and a larger society that is insufficiently defined."[15]

The defining of the centre, vital for social cohesion, is a guiding principle that goes beyond bromide. It has been fleshed out, for instance, by Quebec's Superior Council of Education which, in a report released in December 1993, "urged Quebec schools to take charge of introducing immigrant children from many countries to the fundamental values of Quebec society."[16] Pointing out that "old-stock francophones need to understand the rules of the game in a Quebec that is being altered by new waves of immigration," Council president Robert Bisaillon offered elements of the "common public culture" into which immigrants must be integrated:

* French as the official language

* A Judeo-Christian cultural tradition inspired by French, British, American and aboriginal sources
* A legal system based on British common law and French civil law, along with a charter of rights
* A parliamentary democracy based on freedom and equality of citizens
* Respect for the anglophone minority
* An economic system that includes private enterprise and state-operated companies

The newcomer—particularly the non-white, non-francophone, non-Catholic—still occupies an uncertain place in Quebec. Integration is no easier in the streets of Montreal than elsewhere. Racial and linguistic tensions persist. Although the province has been making a concerted effort to move from—in Michael Ignatieff's terms—ethnic (and so exclusive) to civic (and so inclusive) nationalism, the change is not always obvious on June 24, St.-Jean-Baptiste Day, the day of Quebec's "*fête nationale.*"

The reason is this: for some minorities, a majority nationalism on the march is always a fearful sight. The crowds, even though joyous, can be unsettling. The St.-Jean-Baptiste Parade, organized by the St.-Jean-Baptiste Society (the SSJB), underscores the essentially white, francophone, Catholic nature of the province—and for minorities, at least, for those not obviously of the family, it is worrisome to see the easy commingling of language, religion and politics when nationalist politicians head the march organized by the nationalist religious society. The picture, then, is of ethnic solidarity: a picture, for minorities, of exclusion. Although many, maybe most, Quebecers would reject such a restrictive definition of themselves, it remains the message of the massive march every June 24. The fear may not be justified, but dealing with it will require effort on both sides: an effort at inclusion, an effort at adhesion. It is the St.-Jean-Baptiste Parade, with its revelation of emotion, that shows me how far Quebec and those of us not born to the family still have to go.

It must be said, though, that despite the activities of the Front de Libération du Québec in the 1960s—a violence appalling to most Quebecers—Québécois nationalism has been strikingly benign when compared to nationalisms elsewhere. Quebecers are not a violent people. Like other Canadians, they evince a distaste for hatred. There is sincerity in the absurd separatist line that says, "I do not want to destroy your country of Canada. I simply want to build my country of Québec." This is on the whole not a nationalism driven by hatred or a quest for revenge; it is not, with some inevitable exceptions, built on negatives. It is, instead, a sense of the self that allows most Quebecers, separatist or not, to be nationalist without being exclusionary. This could change, but at this point in what is an evolving nationalism, I believe it to be true.

For this reason, then, there is at least the sense that full integration of newcomers into a redefined mainstream may one day be possible. It is from the terms of this self-examination—the sense of limits, the rejection of xenophobia—that vital lessons can be drawn by the country as a whole. As the White Paper further stated: "Between slow or brusque assimilation, and preservation of original characteristics confined within the walls of segregation, there is another practicable road, that of exchanges within a Quebec culture."

And within, let it be said, a Canadian culture.

The view is not alien to us. It was expressed over two decades ago by the Royal Commission on Bilingualism and Biculturalism. In a section remarkable for its understanding of the place of the individual within a shifting social context, the report stated:

> Integration, in the broad sense, does not imply the loss of an individual's identity and original characteristics or of his original language and culture. Man is a thinking and sensitive being; severing him from his roots could destroy an aspect of his personality and deprive society of some of the values he can bring to it. Integration is not synonymous with assimilation. Assimilation implies almost total absorption into another linguistic or cultural group. An assimilated individual gives up his cultural identity, and may even go so far as to change his name. Both integration and assimilation occur in Canada, and the individual must be free to choose whichever process suits him....
>
> The process of integration goes hand in hand with what anthropologists call "acculturation." Anyone who chooses Canada as his adopted country adopts a new style of life, a particular kind of existence.... Acculturation is the process of adaptation to the environment in which an individual is compelled to live as he adjusts his behaviour to that of the community.[17]

We have managed to lose that early and essential view, and in so doing lose ourselves.

The Individual

Not long after leaving Trinidad more than twenty years ago, I received a letter from a respected relative long resident in England. The letter was full of sensible advice that was meant to guide me through the early years of the difficult and exciting journey on which I had embarked.

"Education isn't just doing a course," he wrote. "It is an attitude of mind. Trinidad is behind you, and you have to forget Trinidad and Trinidad attitudes. You have to try to understand the larger world you are now in.... Above all, look about you; look at the landscape, try to enjoy it; try to understand the country and the people, and don't fall into the simple trap of thinking about race all the time."

The letter made it clear that I—like every human being—am part of a vast and ancient human enterprise full of ugliness and beauty. Engage with it, the letter seemed to say; contemplate it; seek to understand as much of it as you possibly can. It was a view that, in the large sense, banished loneliness: knowledge of human history and achievement, it said, was itself a kind of companion.

This country, from the very first, gave me the opportunity to make a start on this sensible advice; and the adventure, engaging both mind and emotion, has tied me to its landscape, its peoples. I remember returning to Toronto from Europe some years ago and standing on my apartment balcony staring out at a sparkling, late-summer evening. I was fresh from the excitements of London and Madrid and Barcelona, but I was taken by the freshness of the air, the pure blue of the sky, the subtle drama of the shifting light. And as I looked out at the familiar buildings of downtown, I knew, in ways I could not define, that it was good to be home. It was a new and remarkable feeling to me.

I have lived in Canada for over twenty years, longer than I have lived anywhere else. I have built a life and a career here. I know who I am, know my autobiography, am at ease with it. But I also know that the specifics of my personality did not freeze, upon my arrival in Toronto, into a form suitable for multicultural display. Migration—the act of leaving, the act of reestablishment—creates its own experience, effects its own change. One is no longer simply who one was in the first part of one's life. To pretend that one has not evolved, as official multiculturalism so often seems to demand of us, is to stultify the personality, creating stereotype, stripping the individual of uniqueness: you are not yourself, you are your group. It is not really a mosaic that one joins—the parts of a mosaic fit neatly together, creating a harmonious whole—but rather a zoo of exoticism that one enters. Some are scandalized to speechlessness when I mention that the Trinidad Carnival leaves me unmoved, that I never pine for sandy beaches. Stereotype comforts; its demise disorients. But how wearying it can become.

An unusual view of the discomfort of exoticism was presented in *The Globe and Mail* in November 1993 by a woman named Sherrill Johnson.[18] At the time a graduate student working in developing countries, she wrote of the special treatment she received in India and Guyana by virtue of her exoticism: being a white foreigner in a non-white land opened doors, afforded ease of access denied to others. At the time, engrossed in her work, she unhesitantly accepted the special treatment, and it was only after her return to anonymity in Canada that unease set in. "It's disturbing being singled out on the basis of one's appearance," she wrote, "receiving special favours based on nothing more than the colour of my skin ..." In Guyana, she was called "white meat" in the streets: "[T]he label that I was tagged with started to chafe and it became harder and harder to forget, or perhaps more accurately ignore, the effects of my skin colour—both positive and negative. I longed to walk down a street and not be seen as a blond white woman, or as a piece of 'white meat,' but simply as an ordinary person. Nothing more and nothing less."

The struggle against stereotype, the basis of all racism, is, in the end, a profoundly personal one. Government programs are essential, but no bureaucratic regime can ever be as effective a stop to stereotype and racist type-casting as an immediate challenge by those who object.

At the same time, to accept the assigned role of multiculturalism—to play the ethnic deracinated and costumed—is to play to stereotype. It is to abdicate one's full humanity in favour of one of its exotic features, ethnicity.

Multiculturalism is ethnicity as public policy: it is society's view of the individual's assigned place within its construct. And yet I would suggest that ethnicity's true value lies in the opposite point of view: as one of the many elements that inform the way the individual views the world.

The multicultural society has tended to diminish the role and autonomy of the individual by insisting on placing individuals within preconceived, highly stereotypical confines. It has confused the positive role that ethnicity—one's racial, cultural and historical background(s)—can play in creating the fullness of the self.

In spring 1994, the Montreal *Mirror* ran a short article detailing some of my hesitations about multiculturalism. A printed response came from a man suspicious of my hesitations. He explained that, before multiculturalism, he had had no sense of self, no sense of what he was and where he came from; he had known nothing of his cultural background, and had never been taught his ancestral language. Multiculturalism, he felt, had rectified all that. This echoes a remark Myrna Kostash once made to me; she felt that multiculturalism, by officially recognizing the experience and particularities of "Ukrainian-

Canadians," had validated her own existence in Canada: such explicit recognition of her exoticism, her otherness, was clearly a comfort to her.

This is understandable, and yet unsettling: that we have in this country people who depend on government policy to shore up, to validate, at times even to create their sense of self and of community. It speaks of a startling dependence on government and public policy. I couldn't help wondering about the upbringing of the young man who, before multiculturalism, held himself to be culturally deprived: where, I wondered, were his parents and family through all of this? Was it the role of the state to provide him with a knowledge of his familial past and his ancestral language? It was, it seemed to me, a question of responsibilities—and how much easier it is to point the finger at a distant state than at loved ones.

Perhaps encouraged by the Charter of Rights and Freedoms, we are increasingly jealous of our individual rights. We insist that the state keep its hands out of our personal affairs: My sex life is my own, we say, for instance. Yet so many of us seem to depend on the state for the sense of self that comes from official recognition of our cultural background. Is this not a kind of psychic surrender?

Heritage belongs first and foremost to the individual. It seems to me possible to instruct an individual child in his or her cultural heritage without erecting ghetto walls by engaging in communal endeavour. Emphasizing the "I" and de-emphasizing the "we" may be the only way to avoid the development of cultural chauvinism, the idea that "we" are superior to "them," and the chasms that result. It is possible to shape a child whose outlook is informed by the knowledge of a certain cultural, familial past, by pride in a Canadian present and by hope in a Canadian future.

My own daughter will grow up knowing her families, seeing the photos of those now dead, hearing the stories of a distant past. She will know of her Québécois great-grandfather who went to war and returned damaged. She will know of her Trinidadian great-grandfather who began life in poverty and ended it in wealth. She will hear of the grandmothers she never knew. She will be acquainted with the varied streams of history that have come together to create her, at this particular time, in this particular place. She will be acquainted, then, with her heritage: that body of knowledge that firmly plants the individual; the body of knowledge that requires no particular soil, no particular air; the body of knowledge that is like freedom because it can be carried safely through time and space in the capacious pocket of the mind, as orienting as a compass; the body of knowledge, then, that no one can ever steal or play with or manipulate into the service of social engineering. Personal knowledge and sensitivities are media for growth. They are not the basis for public policy.

Multiculturalism, on the face of it, insists on diversity—and yet a case can be made that it is a diversity that depends on a vigorous conformity. Trading in the exotic, it views the individual not as a member of society at large but as a unit of a smaller group ethnically, racially or culturally defined—a group comforted by the knowledge that it has access to familiar foods, music, etc. But this is multiculturalism at its most simplistic, and in some ways most insidious, level. It is the trade-off of the marketplace, an assurance of creature comforts in exchange for playing the ethnic game. The same comforts can be had from any decent New York City supermarket—and at a price far less demanding.

There is no need to abandon that which has been, to devalue that which is or to fear that which can be—no need for rigidly defined ethnicities or for divided loyalties, no space for government to tell anyone who he or she is. This, then, is the direction in which we should be heading: towards the recognition that heritage, in the end, belongs only to the individual—and where aspects of heritage conflict, dialogue must ensue, compromise sought for the good not only of the individuals involved but of the larger society as well.

Citizenship

> *I swear (or affirm) that I will be faithful and bear true allegiance to Her Majesty Queen Elizabeth the Second, Queen of Canada, Her Heirs and Successors, and that I will faithfully observe the laws of Canada and fulfill my duties as a Canadian citizen.*
>
> Citizenship Act

Citizenship is about inclusion. The desire for it emerges from the realization that one's intellectual and emotional loyalties have, through the years, come to commit themselves to the idea and actuality of Canada. One makes a life, puts down roots, and from this feeling of belonging comes the wish to be as fully part of the country as possible.

A friend had set me at ease about the first part of the citizenship process. It was simple, he said. Answer a few rudimentary questions about the country, display a grasp of the language, chat a bit with the kindly examiner (this job, he intimated, was their pasture) and watch as he or she signs your papers with a flourish worthy of royalty. And, hell, even those rules weren't hard and fast: his own aged mother had spent over twenty years in

Toronto, had managed to acquire none of the language, but had nevertheless been granted citizenship by a kindly examiner sympathetic to her wish to die as a citizen of the country that had been good to her family.

And, indeed, it was as my friend had said: the simple questions, the friendly banter, the regal flourish. He could not have predicted, though, that my sprightly examiner would urge me not to abuse the too-expensive health-care system or that he would slip in a good word for the NDP.

The second step, three months later, was slightly more difficult, if only because it veered so close to farce.

We were a large and suitably multicultural group, strangers gathered in the solemnity of a courtroom by our impending citizenship. After an uneasy wait, we were treated to a lengthy speech by the citizenship judge, resplendent in a gown of billowing black silk. He was a man of dignity and a certain friendly charm, but there was a problem: his Italian accent was so heavy one could hardly begin to guess at the pearls of wisdom he was trying to transmit to us. The mind wandered, speculating on what an achievement it must have been for him to fulfill the language qualification during his own citizenship exam. Amidst the stirring and the coughing, one could feel the solemnity dissipate. This man was supposed to be swearing us in. For all we knew, he might have been simply swearing.

Finally, we chorused the oath of citizenship, which was followed by a rendition of "O Canada," everyone standing with gaze directed, as instructed, towards a colour photograph on the wall, the dress-uniformed Mountie ramrod-stiff as he directed a salute towards the same photo, of Elizabeth II, Queen of Canada. It seemed, as we worked our way through the words familiar from hockey games, a kind of idolatry.

There was no cheering at the end, no sense of occasion as we, at the urging of the judge, shyly shook each other's hands in congratulations. And then we were free of the courtroom, back out in the street among the traffic, changed by the papers that attested to our new status but hurrying back to jobs and obligations with a curious sense of anticlimax. It was a while before elation came to me, but it did. And it came with the realization that at the next election I too would be joining the line at a polling station. The citizenship examination and ceremony might have been exercises in comedy, but it was, like the best comedy, comedy with purpose.

And it was with purpose that in April 1994, Immigration Minister Sergio Marchi announced a prospective reform of the citizenship process. Along with a streamlining of the process, Mr. Marchi announced the abolishment of citizenship judges. The post, a patronage appointment, pays an average of $65,000 per year to fifty or so people. It has never required much in the way of qualification. In 1993, the Mulroney cabinet appointed a close friend of the prime minister's wife; the woman doubled her salary and traded in her receptionist's chair for the splendour of a judge's bench. In 1985, the mother of present deputy prime minister Sheila Copps, appointed by the Trudeau government, was removed by the Conservatives. In 1987, two Conservative appointees were accused of urging new citizens to vote Tory; the senior citizenship judge, instructed to review the competence of the judges, withdrew from the review after it was revealed that she herself was a longtime Conservative and had once been chief of staff to a cabinet minister. Even former prime minister Brian Mulroney once characterized the judgeships as "a bit of a boondoggle"[19]—and no one knows a boondoggle better than Brian Mulroney.

In proposing his reforms, Mr. Marchi stated that his aim was in large measure "to evoke a feeling of national pride and belonging in society."[20] It is a laudable aim, but it strikes me as evocative of the old cliché of the cart and the horse.

At the moment, through our multiculturalism policy, we encourage a feeling of *ethnic* pride and belonging in *narrowed communities.* Replacing the comedy of the citizenship process with a ceremony that would observe an appropriate solemnity, while laudable in vision, is much too little, much too late. That "feeling of national pride and belonging" will not suddenly blossom splendidly at the ceremonies voluntarily presided over by Order of Canada recipients in local church basements, school gyms and community halls. That feeling must start well before; it must take root and grow in the years of establishment leading up to the commitment of citizenship—but this will not happen so long as immigrants are made to understand that the culture they encounter here pales before the one that accompanies them.

Just as a marriage ceremony is the public celebration of a love that already exists, so citizenship ceremonies must be the celebration of a feeling of national pride and belonging that already exists. Multiculturalism, with its emphasis on the ethnic and not the national, on fealty to the cultural community rather than to the society at large, works hard at defeating Mr. Marchi's grand purpose. It is indisputable that reform of the citizenship process is vital. But citizenship marks the end of the immigrant journey. Reform of multiculturalism, which comes at the beginning of that journey, is even more vital.

It may be that one of the unstated desires behind the institution of multiculturalism was a wish to mark ourselves as different fron the United States: If they have a melting pot, then we'll have a mosaic. If they ask immigrants to shrug off their past and assume a new identity, we'll ask immigrants to conserve their past and make it their only identity.

Both approaches are essentially illusory, it seems to me, each an exercise in the falsifying of the self. Pretending to continue being simply what one has been in the past, or what one's parents have been, inevitably entails a betrayal of the self—just as pretending, under the assimilative American model, that one is no longer what one has been, that one has completely remade oneself, is also a betrayal of the self. The human personality is not static; it is altered fundamentally, but not wholly, by circumstance and experience. And while the U.S. approach is untrue to the individual, the Canadian approach is untrue to both the individual and the state. For if many who immigrate to the United States eventually come to think of themselves as simply "American," strengthening the social fabric, too few who come to Canada end up accepting themselves—and one another—as simply "Canadian," thereby weakening the social fabric.

A middle way must be found, a route that establishes, as Quebec is attempting to do, certain basic social parameters to which all must dedicate themselves and within which one is free to live as one wishes.

It is time we removed personal culture and ethnicity from the manipulative realm of public policy and returned it to individuals and their families, the only sphere where they have any true and lasting value. As a young television producer of Indian background once remarked: "I don't need some bureaucrat in Ottawa to tell me who I am." Society has sufficient reasonable expectations of its citizens. Let us cease adding to them unreasonable ones.

In his book *The New Canada*, Preston Manning offers an excerpt from a presentation made to the Reform Party by professor Rais Khan, chair of the political science department at the University of Winnipeg. It is a statement that lays bare the creed of the immigrant and points the way to Bharati Mukherjee's exuberance of immigration:

> People, regardless of their origin, do not emigrate to preserve their culture and nurture their ethnic distinctiveness. If they wished to do that, they would stay where they were because the environment is more conducive to the perpetuation of one's culture and ethnicity. Immigrants come here to become Canadians; to be productive and contributing members of their chosen society. I am one of them. I did not come here to be labelled as an ethnic or a member of the multicultural community, or to be coddled with preferential treatment, nurtured with special grants, and then to sit on the sidelines and watch the world go by. I came here to be a member of the mainstream of the Canadian society. I do not need paternalism; I need opportunity. I do not want affirmative action; I expect fairness. I do not desire special consideration; I wish to be treated equally.... Whether or not I preserve my cultural background is my personal choice; whether or not an ethnic group preserves its cultural background is the group's choice. The state has no business in either.[21]

They who wish to divide are legion, but so too are we who wish to belong.

In an article in *The Globe and Mail* on July 18, 1991, Dr. Suwanda Sugunasiri, a former member of the Ontario Advisory Council on Multiculturalism and Citizenship, called for the abolition of the federal secretary of state's multiculturalism directorate and proposed that its functions be incorporated into the Ministry of Culture and Communications, with an emphasis on countering racism. He called for the disbanding of multicultural advisory councils, an end to heritage-language programs and the abolition of the monarchy (which he dubbed a racist institution). Pointing to an Angus Reid poll which suggested that only one in ten Canadians supported multiculturalism, he indicated that the policy, which he characterized as having entered its adolescence, had, in its present form, outlived its usefulness. As he pointed out, the policy "was useful in giving multicultural communities a presence, but we know they're there now."

Certainly, at this point in our social development (or lack of it), ethnic communities have little to gain from multiculturalism, a policy that now serves to make them, more than anything else, simply privy to political manipulation from both inside and outside their communities.

Furthermore, indulging in the game of heightened ethnicity entails the risk of excessive fantasy. It is human to edit the past, to gloss even a harsh reality into a coveted memory: "We were starving, but we were happy." But such memory of a retreating past ever more golden frequently leads to acute personal dissatisfaction. It is easy, in the comforting grip of edited memory, to forget that everything has changed; easy, too, to embrace the miscalculation that arises from an acute yearning for the perfection that, in memory, used to be. Multiculturalism, with its stress on the theatrical, helps concretize such fantasy, and once more both the individual and the state lose—the one by clinging to and at times acting on a fantasy, the other by paling before golden fantasy taken for reality.

In his article, Dr. Sugunasiri suggests several ways in which minority communities can help in "building a just society." He warns against "crying racism at every turn" and urges that they "look inward at the racism and discrimination within [their] own ranks." He encourages them to seek greater co-operation with legal authorities and calls for an effort to "get rid of the dehumanizing aspects" of their cultures. He also insists that historical injustices be left in the past, that they not be allowed to poison the present and, thus, the future—an elegant way of pleading with people to get rid of the chips on their shoulders. Finally, Dr. Sugunasiri offers what seems a radical policy: "Intermarriage must be promoted; it's perhaps our best hope for security and stability. More than 32 per cent of Canadians are the products of mixed marriages; the Japanese-Canadian figure is 50 per cent. Rejuvenate the gene pool."

While I endorse many of Dr. Sugunasiri's suggestions, I would not go as far as he does in his final recommendation. So long as it does not adversely affect others, what people do in their private lives is their own business, whether it be what food they choose to eat, which foreign languages and heritage dances they choose to teach their children or whom they choose to marry. State intervention in private affairs (as opposed to, say, intervention in private companies engaged in profit-making through public enterprise) is rarely benign.

In her brief tenure as prime minister, Kim Campbell reduced multiculturalism from a full department to a dossier. Dr. Sugunasiri recommends its full abolition, but this is a task that, despite the unpopularity of the policy and because of the influence of interest groups, might prove politically risky for any government. In the face of this reality, the entire sphere of multiculturalism should at the very least be removed from the political arena. It should either be incorporated into the Ministry of Culture and Communications, as suggested, or established as an arm's-length agency of the federal government, in the manner of the Canada Council, funded by the government but not controlled by it.

Its budget, which is neither overwhelming nor insignificant, could be put to far better use than the building of community halls and social facilities for specific, ethnically defined groups. The bulk of its funds should be allocated instead to battling racism. Aiming to establish understanding and inclusion, seeking to diminish racism by exposing Canadians to other Canadians, the government should concentrate on funding school or community programs that sensitize children to each other, stressing not the differences that divide them but the similarities that unite them.

Despite the varying pasts that have shaped us, we are all in the final analysis Canadians, with a common country and common interests that can, if permitted, lead to a common future. Children of Serbian and children of Croatian descent, for instance, might come to realize that here, in this country, they have more to gain by leaving aside Old World feuds than by joining in them. They might come to realize that Canada really does provide a second chance—but that it is up to them to take advantage of it.

In October 1978, the accomplished journalist and feminist Laura Sabia addressed the Empire Club of Canada. She said in part:

> I was born and bred in this amazing land. I've always considered myself a Canadian, nothing more, nothing less, even though my parents

> were immigrants from Italy. How come...we have all acquired a hyphen? We have allowed ourselves to become divided along the lines of ethnic origins, under the pretext of the "Great Mosaic." A dastardly deed has been perpetrated upon Canadians by politicians whose motto is "divide and rule." I, for one, refuse to be hyphenated. I am a Canadian, first and foremost. Don't hyphenate me.[22]

With this as a guiding vision, whatever may come after multiculturalism will aim not at preserving differences but at blending them into a new vision of Canadianness, pursuing a Canada where inherent differences and inherent similarities meld easily and where no one is alienated with hyphenation. A nation of cultural hybrids, where every individual is unique, every individual distinct. And every individual is Canadian, undiluted and undivided.

The ultimate goal, then, is a cohesive, effective society enlivened by cultural variety: reasonable diversity within vigorous unity. We already have the first. Now we must seek the second, even if that would mean—as it must—a certain diminishment of the first.

What remains to be decided is whether we have the will, individually and collectively, to summon a new vision—or whether we wish to continue, as we have been, purchasing the illusions of this "false and nation-sapping god."[23]

Endnotes

Chapter One: Glimpses Beneath the Surface

1 Jack Kapica, "Canadians want mosaic to melt, survey finds: Respondents believe immigrants should adopt Canada's values," *The Globe and Mail*, December 14, 1993.

2 Allyson Jeffs (Southam News), "Canadians Harbor 'Latently Racist' Attitudes: Poll," December 14, 1993.

3 Murray Campbell, "Too Many Immigrants, Many Say," *The Globe and Mail*, March 10, 1994.

4 For Vancouver, the figure was 51 percent (up 2 points in two years); and for Montreal 39 percent (up 10 points in two years)—a figure that strikes a serious blow against the widespread belief in Québécois intolerance.

5 Terrance Wills, "Visible-Minority Liberals criticize BQ, Reform over 'ghetto' remark," *Montreal Gazette*, January 29, 1994.

Chapter Three: Beginnings

1 Quoted in John Robert Colombo, ed., *The Dictionary of Canadian Quotations* (Toronto: Stoddart, 1991), p. 339.

2 Michael Ignatieff, *The Russian Album* (London: Chatto & Windus Ltd., 1987), p. 158.

3 *Ibid.*, p. 163.

4 Conversation with Michael Ignatieff, Montreal, December 1, 1993.

5 *Ibid.*

6 Ramsay Cook, "The Triumph and Trials of Materialism," in *The Illustrated History of Canada* (Toronto: Lester & Orpen Dennys, 1987).

7 Glenda P. Simms, "Racism as a Barrier," in *Belonging: The Meaning and Future of Canadian Citizenship*, ed. William Kaplan (Montreal: McGill-Queen's University Press, 1993), p. 337.

8 *Ibid.*, p. 391.

9 Irving Abella and Harold Troper, *None is Too Many* (Toronto: Lester Publishing, 1991), pp. xxii-xxiii.

10 Ken Adachi, *The Enemy that Never Was* (Toronto: McClelland & Stewart, 1976).

11 Richard Gwyn, *The Northern Magus* (Toronto: McClelland & Stewart, 1980), p. 139.

12 René Lévesque, quoted in Colombo, *The Dictionary of Canadian Quotations.*

13 Christian Dufour, *Le Défi québécois* (Montréal: l'Hexagone, 1989), p. 77 (my translation).

Chapter Four: Losing the Centre

1 "Legion Bars Sikh Veterans," *The Globe and Mail*, Canadian Press, November 12, 1993.

2 Deborah Wilson, "Legion HQ Apologizes for B.C. Turban Row," *The Globe and Mail*, November 13, 1993.

3 Quoted in Michael Valpy, "When the Legion Withholds its Welcome," *The Globe and Mail*, January 7, 1994.

4 "Legion says no to bylaw allowing religious headgear," *Montreal Gazette*, June 1, 1994.

5 "Veterans visit Italian battleground," *The Globe and Mail*, May 16, 1994.

6 Katherine Bell, "Lawyers in turban case argue over religious symbols in public life," Canadian Press, *Montreal Gazette*, April 23, 1994.

7 Geoff Baker, "Judge draws fire for expelling woman from court," *Montreal Gazette*, December 3, 1993.

8 Alexander Norris, "Muslim woman faces grilling over religion," *Montreal Gazette*, January 8, 1994.

9 "Judge in 'hijab case' declares an abiding admiration for Muslims," *Montreal Gazette*, April 13, 1994.

10 Michael Valpy, "It is a question of judgment," *The Globe and Mail*, February 25, 1994.

11 Michael Valpy, "Haven't they got anything better to do?" *The Globe and Mail*, November 30, 1993.

12 "Christmas decorations allowed," *The Globe and Mail*, November 24, 1993.

13 Wendy Cox, "Santas at Toronto mall are fat, jolly and black, Pakistani and Asian," Canadian Press, *Montreal Gazette*, November 20, 1993.

14 Editorial, *Montreal Gazette*, February 16, 1994.

15 Editorial, *The Globe and Mail*, February 19, 1994.

16 Phillip Day, "Commons gives new prayer its blessing," Canadian Press, *Montreal Gazette*, February 19, 1994.

17 Jack Kapica, "Divide over Christ rises in church body," *The Globe and Mail*, May 17, 1994.

18 Christian Dufour, "A Little History," excerpt from *Le Défi Québécois*, in *Boundaries of Identity*, ed. William Dodge (Toronto: Lester Publishing Ltd., Toronto, 1992).

19 Preston Manning, *The New Canada* (Toronto: Macmillan Canada, 1992), p. 25.

20 *Ibid.*, pp. 272, 273.

21 *Ibid.*, p. 24.

22 *Ibid.*, p. 317.

23 *Ibid.*

24 *Ibid.*, p. 273.

25 Hugh Winsor, "Reform Candidate Quits," *The Globe and Mail*, October 14, 1993.

26 *Ibid.*

27 *Ibid.*

28 "Reform candidate says new immigrants are a burden," Canadian Press, *The Globe and Mail*, October 15, 1993.

29 "Women's, minority groups called 'parasites' by Reform official," Canadian Press, *The Globe and Mail*, October 29, 1993.

30 William D. Gairdner, *The Trouble with Canada* (Toronto: General Paperbacks, 1991).

31 *Ibid.*, p. 81.

32 *Ibid.*

33 *Ibid.*, p. 397.

34 *Ibid.*, p. 272.

35 *Ibid.*, p. 281.

36 *Ibid.*

37 *Ibid.*, p. 78.

38 *Ibid.*, p. 414.

39 *Ibid.*, p. 412.

40 *Ibid.*, p. 411.

41 *Ibid.*, p. 393; James Fallows, "Asia: Nobody Wants a Melting Pot,"

U.S. News & World Report, June 22, 1987.

42 Michael Valpy, "A fear of losing the old Canada," *The Globe and Mail*, March 11, 1994.

43 *Ibid.*

44 Sadanand Joshi, "Canadian values," letter to *The Globe and Mail*, March 22, 1994.

45 Murray Campbell, "Too Many Immigrants, Many Say," *The Globe and Mail*, March 10, 1994.

46 "Royal visit to Bahamas draws little enthusiasm," Reuter, *Montreal Gazette*, March 8, 1994.

47 Michael Valpy, "A fear of losing the old Canada."

48 Michael Valpy, "Haven't they got anything better to do?" *The Globe and Mail*, November 30, 1993.

Chapter Five: The Simplification of Culture

1 V.S. Naipaul, *A Bend in the River* (New York: Alfred A. Knopf, 1979), p. 3.

2 Irwin Block, "Women outraged by judge's remarks," *Montreal Gazette*, January 15, 1994.

3 Geoff Baker, "Stepdad gets 2 years in sex assault," *Montreal Gazette*, January 14, 1994.

4 *The Globe and Mail*, November 12, 1993.

5 *Ibid.*

6 *Ibid.*

7 Margot Gibb-Clark, "Ontario stage set for job equity," *The Globe and Mail*, November 24, 1993.

8 "Examination by disadvantage?" editorial, *The Globe and Mail*, February 19, 1994.

Chapter Six: The Uses of Ethnicity

1 Lynda Hurst, "Coloring crime stats by race," *Toronto Star*, November 27, 1993.

2 *Ibid.*

3 *Ibid.*

4 *Ibid.*

5 *Ibid.*

6 Joy Kogawa, in *Cultures and Writers: A Cultural Dialogue of Ethnic*

Writers, ed. Yvonne Grabowski, in *The Dictionary of Canadian Quotations*, ed. John Robert Colombo (Toronto: Stoddart, 1991).

7 Trinidad-born novelist (A *Brighter Sun, The Lonely Londoners*); lived for many years in London before moving to Calgary. He died suddenly in April 1994, while on a visit to Trinidad. He was 71.

8 Novelist (*The Tiger's Daughter, Wife, Jasmine*) and short-story writer (*Darkness, The Middleman and Other Stories*, which won the 1988 [U.S.] National Book Critics Circle Award).

9 Short-story writer (*Tales from Firozsha Baag*) and novelist (*Such a Long Journey*, which won numerous prizes including the Governor General's Award).

10 Screenwriter (*My Beautiful Laundrette, Sammy and Rosie Get Laid*) and novelist (*The Buddha of Suburbia*).

11 Salman Rushdie, "Imaginary Homelands," in *Imaginary Homelands*, Granta Books in assoc. with Penguin Books, 1991, pp. 16-17.

12 Robert Matas, "Minister loathes ethnic politics," *The Globe and Mail*, January 8, 1994.

13 Robert Matas, "A 'banana' split in Vancouver," *The Globe and Mail*, February 25, 1994.

14 *Ibid.*

15 *Ibid.*

16 *Ibid.*

17 Bharati Mukherjee, *Darkness* (Toronto: Penguin, 1985), pp. 1-2.

18 *Ibid.*, p. 2.

19 *Ibid.*

20 Mukherjee, *Darkness*, p. 2.

21 Toronto: McClelland & Stewart Ltd, 1992.

22 V.S. Naipaul, *A Bend in the River* (New York: Alfred A. Knopf, 1979), p. 236 .

23 Naipaul, pp. 236-237.

24 Colombo, p. 72.

25 Colombo, p. 251.

26 Iona Monahan, "Ethné and Trudi: sisters in style," *Montreal Gazette*, February 22, 1994.

27 Ali Sharrif, "Caught in a strange racial divide," *The Globe and Mail*, September 21, 1993.

28 *Ibid.* In an article for *NOW* some months later, Sharrif detailed

the sorry fate of the African Community Health Services (ACHES), which had been the object of a battle for control between its founders (Ugandans and Kenyans linked by a common language, Swahili) and challengers from the Eritrean and Somali communities ("two relatively closely related cultural groups"). There were accusations of ethnic favouritism, of stacked meetings, of demands for "inclusion" as a mere excuse for personal political ambition. The Eritrean/Somali faction won, and Toronto's African community, some 100,000 strong, was radically split. Ethnicity, too, has its fissures.

29 "MPP won't apologize," *The Globe and Mail*, Dec. 7, 1991.

30 David Remnick, "Belfast Confetti," *The New Yorker*, April 25, 1994, p. 64.

31 Dana Milbank, "Latvia not majestic place of parents' dreams," *The Wall Street Journal, The Globe and Mail*, January 8, 1994.

32 Michael Ignatieff, *Blood and Belonging* (Toronto: Viking, 1993), p. 82.

33 Thomas Keneally, *Schindler's List* (New York: Simon and Schuster, 1982), p. 379.

34 Nino Ricci, interview, *Profiles* magazine, February, 1994.

35 V.S. Naipaul, *An Area of Darkness* (London: Andre Deutsch Limited, 1964), p. 266.

36 *Ibid.*, p. 273.

37 *Ibid.*, p. 276.

38 *Ibid.*, pp. 279-280.

39 Ignatieff, *Blood and Belonging*, pp. 106-107.

40 Salman Rushdie, *Imaginary Homelands*, p. 19.

Chapter Seven: The Limits of Diversity

1 Sherri Davis Barron, "Doctors draw up policy on female circumcision," *Toronto Star*, January 6, 1992.

2 Christine Hodge, "Throwing away the circumcision knife," *The Globe and Mail*, January 15, 1994.

3 *NOW* magazine, Toronto, January 27–February, 1994.

4 Sean Fine, "End sought to mandatory charges in wife-abuse cases," *The Globe and Mail*, January 27, 1994.

5 Cecil Foster, "All black schools: more ghettoes?" *The Globe and Mail*, September, 30, 1993.

6 Quoted in "Visible Man," an article on Ralph Ellison, by David Remnick, *The New Yorker*, March 14, 1994, p. 38.

7 *The Globe and Mail*, April 13, 1994.

8 See James Traub, "Can Separate Be Equal?" *Harper's*, June 1994.

Chapter Eight: Diversity and Creativity

1 Salman Rushdie, *Imaginary Homelands*, p. 20.

2 Alice Munro, "Labour Day Dinner" in *The Moons of Jupiter* (Toronto: Penguin Books, 1986), p. 150.

3 Roch Carrier, "The Hockey Sweater," trans. by Sheila Fischman, in *Breaking Through*, ed. John Borovilos (Toronto: Prentice-Hall, 1990).

4 Alberto Manguel, "To deny the past is worse than foolish," *The Globe and Mail*, April 28, 1994.

5 Bernie M. Farber, "Merchant of Venice has made young Jewish students suffer," *Montreal Gazette*, November 5, 1993.

6 Even the term "Jew" is problematic. Centuries of anti-Semitism have made it a term of abuse, so that popular sensitivities now prefer to refer to "Jewish persons." I found myself reassured, though, while listening to a speech by former Israeli defence minister Ariel Sharon, who had no hesitation in referring to himself as a Jew, to his people as Jews. While some will choose to see this, particularly from Sharon, as a mark of belligerence, I prefer to see it as a sign of pride: to allow the word to be expropriated by hate-mongers is to betray a little part of yourself.

7 "School ban urged for Steinbeck novel," *The Globe and Mail*, March 2, 1994.

8 Portia Priegert, "MP was wrong to quote Hitler in newsletter: Manning," Canadian Press, *Montreal Gazette*, February 10, 1994.

9 *Ibid.*

10 M. Nourbese Philip, "Immoral Fiction" in *Frontiers* (Stratford: The Mercury Press, 1992), p. 190.

11 M. Nourbese Philip, "Publish + Be Damned" in *Frontiers*, p. 162.

12 See Adele Freedman, "White Woman's Burden," *Saturday Night*, April 1993.

13 M. Nourbese Philip, "Disturbing the Peace" in *Frontiers*, p. 135.

14 Robert Fulford, "The ongoing assault on academic freedom," *The Globe and Mail*.

15 Susan Crean, "Taking the Missionary Position," *The Broadview Reader*, 2nd ed., eds. Herbert Rosengarten and Jane Flick, (Peterborough: Broadview Press, 1992).

16 Myrna Kostash, Report from the Chair, in "The Writers' Union of Canada Newsletter," vol. 21, No. 6, December 1993.

17 Robert Fulford, "George Orwell, Call Your Office," *The Globe and Mail*, March 30, 1994.

18 Roy Miki, "Why we're holding the Vancouver conference," *The Globe and Mail*, April 7, 1994.

19 Bronwyn Drainie, "Controversial writers' meeting is both meet and right," *The Globe and Mail*, April 16, 1994.

20 Robert Fulford, "George Orwell, Call Your Office."

21 Val Ross, "Writers Union controversy on hold," *The Globe and Mail*, May 16, 1994

22 See M. Nourbese Philip, "Gut Issues in Babylon" in *Frontiers*, p. 211.

23 Dionne Brand, "Who Can Speak for Whom?" *Brick*, no. 46, summer 1993, p. 19.

24 See for example M. Nourbese Philip, "Gut Issues in Babylon" in *Frontiers*, where she calls for a commitment by the Women's Press "to publish a certain number of books by (minority) authors annually, or by a certain date" (p. 216).

25 Doreen Kimura, "Universities and the thought police," *The Globe and Mail*, June 28, 1993.

26 Robert Fulford, "Defending the Right to be Offensive," *The Globe and Mail*, February 2, 1994.

27 *Ibid.*

28 Mr. Justice John Sopinka, "Free Speech," *Montreal Gazette*, October 30, 1993.

29 Quote by Rosemary Sullivan in "The Private Enterprise," *Brick* magazine, no. 46, summer 1993.

30 Dagmar Novak, An Interview with Dionne Brand, in *On the Edge*, eds. Arthur Haberman and Fran Cohen (Toronto: Oxford University Press, 1993).

31 Val Ross, "Callwood resigns from Writers Union," *The Globe and Mail*, February 16, 1994.

32 Val Ross, "Writers Union controversy on hold," *The Globe and Mail*, May 16, 1994.

Chapter Nine: Endings

1 Lise Bissonnette, "Culture, Politics and Society in Quebec," in *Boundaries of Identity*, ed. William Dodge (Toronto: Lester Publishing, 1992).

2 *La Presse* and the *Montreal Gazette*, June 13, 1994.

3 René Lévesque, *My Quebec*, trans. Gaynor Fitzpatrick (Toronto: Methuen 1979), p. 14.

4 Pierre Elliott Trudeau, Referendum Speech 1980, Paul Sauvé Arena, May 15, 1980, in *Boundaries of Identity*.

5 Lysiane Gagnon, "If you question Quebec sovereignity, you're a skunk at a garden party," *The Globe and Mail*, April 30, 1994.

6 Mario Fontaine, "Si Charest perd, combien restera-t-il de conservateurs?" *La Presse*, September 20, 1993.

7 Philip Authier, "'Real Quebecers' quote has Parti Québecois running damage control," *Montreal Gazette*, January 27, 1994.

8 Claire Rothman, "Quebec's literary fury descends on Albertan," *Montreal Gazette*, January 29, 1994.

9 Hubert Bauch, "Immigrants should have to integrate, Allaire says," *Montreal Gazette*, February 22, 1994.

10 Richard Martineau, "Pour une culture sans drapeau," *Voir*, March 31-April 6, 1994.

11 Lysiane Gagnon, "Why Quebec nationalists boycotted the launch of a book about their hero, René Lévesque," *The Globe and Mail*, November 6, 1993.

12 Lise Bissonnette, "Who Said Anything About Rest?" in *Boundaries of Identity*, p. 232.

13 *Ibid.*

14 René Lévesque, *My Quebec*, extracts from the white paper on cultural development (June 1978), p. 181.

15 Centrale de l'enseignement du Québec, brief to the Bélanger-Campeau Commission, in *Boundaries of Identity*, p. 177.

16 Sarah Scott, "Teach immigrants our values, panel says," *Montreal Gazette*, December 8, 1993.

17 *Royal Commission on Bilingualism and Biculturalism*, Book IV, Ottawa, 1969, pp. 5-6.

18 Sherrill Johnson, "Beyond single, white, female," *The Globe and Mail*, November 15, 1993.

19 Joan Bryden, "Ottawa set to drop citizenship judges," Southam News, *Montreal Gazette*, April 14, 1994.

20 Terence Wills, "Let's push our Canadian identity, minister says," *Montreal Gazette*, April 15, 1994 .

21 Preston Manning, *The New Canada* (Toronto: Macmillan Canada, 1992), p. 316-317.

22 Laura Sabia, quoted in Colombo ed., *The Dictionary of Canadian Quotations.*

23 Keith Spicer, *Montreal Gazette*, March 9, 1989.